AN ILLUSTRATED GUIDE TO FLYING

BARRY SCHIFF

AVIATION SUPPLIES & ACADEMICS, INC.
NEWCASTLE, WASHINGTON

An Illustrated Guide to Flying
by Barry Schiff

Aviation Supplies & Academics, Inc.
7005 132nd Place SE
Newcastle, Washington 98059
asa@asa2fly.com | 425-235-1500 | asa2fly.com

ASA-IGF
ISBN 978-1-61954-401-7

Additional formats available:
eBook EPUB   ISBN 978-1-61954-402-4
eBook PDF   ISBN 978-1-61954-404-8)

Printed in the United States of America
2026   2025   2024   2023   2022   9 8 7 6 5 4 3 2 1

Cover photo: Copyright Diamond Aircraft.

Library of Congress Cataloging-in-Publication Data

Names: Schiff, Barry J., author.
Title: An illustrated guide to flying / Barry Schiff.
Description: Newcastle, Washington : Aviation Supplies & Academics, Inc., [2022] | Includes index.
Identifiers: LCCN 2022035074 | ISBN 9781619544017 (trade paperback) | ISBN 9781619544024 (epub) | ISBN 9781619544048 (pdf)
Subjects: LCSH: Airplanes—Piloting.
Classification: LCC TL710 .S2925 2022 | DDC 629.132/52—dc23/eng/20220906
LC record available at https://lccn.loc.gov/2022035074

*I am grateful that my wife, Dorie's, loving encouragement
was sufficient to overcome my procrastination lest this literary
labor of love might never have been completed.*

CONTENTS

CHAPTER 1
AVIATION HISTORY

THIS IS HOW IT BEGAN • FAMOUS FLIGHTS

THIS IS HOW IT BEGAN. Man looked into the sky and saw birds. People had always been fascinated by flying. The ancient Chinese made drawings of flying contraptions, and there were Arabic fables about flying carpets.

In Greek mythology, Daedalus was a skilled craftsman who equipped his son, Icarus, with wings of wax with which to escape the maze where they had been held captive. Excited by the thrill of flight and contrary to his father's warning, Icarus flew too high, and the heat of the sun caused his wings to melt. He fell from the sky and was swallowed by the sea.

In the fifteenth century, Leonardo da Vinci designed and built a model of a helicopter that presumably flew. His drawings and designs were among the first recorded as practical contributions to human's eventual mastery of flight. He also designed an ornithopter, a machine with flapping wings, but this likely did not fly.

Balloons became the craze in the eighteenth century. Two Frenchmen, the Montgolfier brothers, experimented with paper balloons filled with hot air. They demonstrated their balloon to King Louis XVI and Queen Marie Antoinette. A sheep, a rooster, and a duck were sent aloft in the balloon, which reached 300 feet, proving that life could exist at such a great height.

During a subsequent balloon demonstration, Benjamin Franklin was asked by a bystander, What good is a balloon? What will it accomplish? Franklin famously replied, "Of what value is a new-born baby?"[1]

While balloonists were setting altitude and distance records, attempts were concurrently being made at heavier-than-air flight. A sea captain from Brittany built an artificial albatross with a 23-foot wingspan. It was launched like a kite by a horse-drawn cart. It lifted from the ground until the rope caught the driver and yanked him from the cart. The contraption was forced down by the added weight.

In the late nineteenth century, Otto Lilienthal made many successful glider flights that proved the concept of the wing. He was about to attempt powered flight when he suffered a fatal accident. Inspired by Lilienthal's achievements, the Wright brothers, Orville and Wilbur, began their own work with airplanes in their Dayton, Ohio, bicycle shop. Their progress, however, was delayed due to lack of availability of a sufficiently powerful, lightweight engine. They finally built their own 12-horsepower engine.

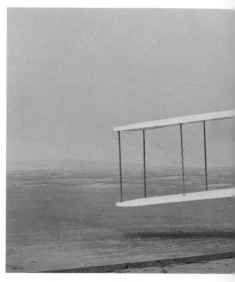

So it was that on a bleak, windy day, December 17, 1903, near Kitty Hawk, North Carolina, that the Wright brothers made their historic flight. Orville modestly said that "this flight lasted only 12 seconds, but it was nevertheless the first...in which a machine carrying a man had raised itself by its own power into the air in full flight, had sailed forward [120 feet] without reduction of speed, and had finally landed at a point as high as that from which it started."[2]

Two years later the Wrights established a record by flying 24 miles, and in 1910, Glenn Curtiss flew 152 miles. In 1911, Cal Rodgers made the first flight across the United States, which took 49 days and included 19 crashes, a record unto itself. By 1914, an airplane had flown over Mount Whitney at 16,000 feet, and with each succeeding year, humankind flew increasingly higher, farther, and faster.

Aviation began to play a more practical if not violent role during World War I. General William "Billy" Mitchell was the first American to fly over enemy lines, and men such as Eddie Rickenbacker, known as "America's Ace of Aces," quickened the public's interest in aviation. When the war ended, the U.S. military had 6,000 surplus airplanes, and there were many wanting to fly them.

In 1918, the U.S. Post Office inaugurated airmail service. At first, Army pilots flew these routes, but civilian pilots eventually replaced them. This early service laid the foundation for our present-day air transportation system. In 1921, the first transcontinental night flight was made with obliging farmers lighting bonfires to serve as beacons.

One of those early airmail pilots was Charles Lindbergh. In 1927, he flew alone from New York to Paris in the *Spirit of St. Louis*, and two continents went into hysterics over it. Lindbergh believed that his flight was a forerunner of an air service between America and Europe that would bring people closer together in understanding and friendship. The Lindbergh flight was adrenalin in the bloodstream of American aviation, and interest in flying exploded.

The 1920s saw the first aircraft built to effectively carry passengers from coast to coast (with many stops)—the Ford Tri-Motor, called the "Tin Goose" because of its corrugated metal skin. The Douglas DC-3 was introduced in the late 1930s and is considered to have been the first modern airliner.

Necessity being the mother of invention, World War II accelerated the advancement of aviation

technology. The war gave rise to giant bombers, near-supersonic fighters, rocket engines, and the birth of the jet age.

What does the future hold for aviation? Will there be hypersonic, suborbital flights between major cities of the world? Passenger flights to celestial destinations? Paraphrasing Napoleon Hill, "Whatever the mind of a man or a woman can conceive and believe, he or she can achieve."[3]

The first successful flight of the Wright Flyer (above).

Charles Lindbergh and the Spirit of St. Louis (left).

FAMOUS FLIGHTS

1783 First manned flight—J.F. Pilâtre de Rozier and the Marquis d'Arlandes in a balloon.

1797 First parachute descent—André J. Garnerin from a balloon over Paris.

1852 First flight in a dirigible—Henri Giffard using a 3 hp steam engine.

1903 First flight in an airplane—Orville Wright above Kill Devil Hills, Kitty Hawk, NC.

1907 First flight of a manned helicopter—Paul Cornu over Normandy, France.

1909 First flight across the English Channel—Louis Blériot in a monoplane of his own design.

1911 First flight across the U.S.—Calbraith Rodgers; the trip took 49 days and included 19 crashes.

1919 First flight across the Atlantic Ocean—Lt. Com. Albert Cushing Read in a Navy Curtiss flying boat.

1919 First nonstop flight across the Atlantic Ocean—John Alcock and Arthur Brown.

1922 First flight across the U.S. in less than a day (21 hr 20 min)—James Doolittle.

1924 First flight around the world—Lts. John Macready and Oakley Kelly in a Douglas World Cruiser.

1926 First flight over the North Pole—Richard Byrd and Floyd Bennett.

1927 First nonstop flight from New York to Paris—Charles Lindbergh in the *Spirit of St. Louis*.

Charles "Chuck" Yeager and the Bell X-1 *Glamorous Glennis* in which he made the first supersonic flight.

Wiley Post and *Winnie Mae.*

1927 First flight from California to Hawaii—Lester Maitland and Albert Hegenberger.
1929 First "blind" takeoff and landing using instruments only—James Doolittle.
1932 First transatlantic flight by a woman—Amelia Earhart.
1933 First solo flight around the world Wiley Post in the *Winnie Mae.*
1937 Amelia Earhart disappeared during her attempted flight around the world.
1938 Howard Hughes and his crew set an around-the-world speed record of 3 days 19 hours.
1938 In a Curtiss Robin, Douglas "Wrong Way" Corrigan purported to go west from New York and instead headed in the opposite direction, ending up in Ireland.
1939 First flight of a jet powered airplane—the Heinkel He-178 at Rostock, Germany.
1947 The first supersonic flight—Charles Yeager in the Bell X-1 rocket plane.
1954 The author of this book made his first solo flight.
1969 First manned flight to the surface of the moon—Neil Armstrong, Buzz Aldrin, and Michael Collins.
1976 Fastest speed ever attained in a jet-powered airplane—2,193 mph in a Lockheed SR-71 "Blackbird."
1981 First launch of the Space Shuttle.
1986 First nonstop flight around the world without refueling—Dick Rutan and Jeana Yeager in the Rutan Voyager.
1999 First nonstop flight around the world in a balloon (19 days 2 hrs)—Brian Jones and Bertrand Piccard in the *Breitling Orbiter 3.*

CHAPTER 2
THE SCIENCE OF FLIGHT

THE ATMOSPHERE • ATMOSPHERIC PRESSURE AND TEMPERATURE
AIRSPEED AND AIR PRESSURE • LIFT • DRAG • THRUST • AIRCRAFT DESIGN
FLIGHT CONTROLS • STABILITY • TRIMMING • RELATIVE WIND
ANGLE OF ATTACK • STALLS • FLAPS • TURNS

Flying is possible because of some inherent principles of science that operate in the world in which we live. We do not create these principles; we only use them. Because the atmosphere is the medium in which we fly, we need to begin with some important things to know about the atmosphere.

THE ATMOSPHERE is an ocean of air enveloping the Earth. It provides our lungs with life-supporting oxygen and our aircraft with the necessary support for flight. This air-ocean extends upward for many miles, thinning as it goes higher. There is no exact upper limit to the atmosphere, but it is considered to extend a few hundred miles above the Earth. However, 99 percent of it is less than 20 miles above sea level. If we were to compare the Earth and its atmosphere to an apple and its skin, the skin is 20 times thicker relative to the size of the apple than the atmosphere is to the size of the Earth.

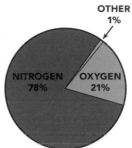

A given volume of pure, dry air contains about 78% nitrogen, 21% oxygen, and a 1% mixture of 11 other gases. Air also can contain water vapor, which varies from 0 to 5% by volume and takes the place of an equal volume of dry air.

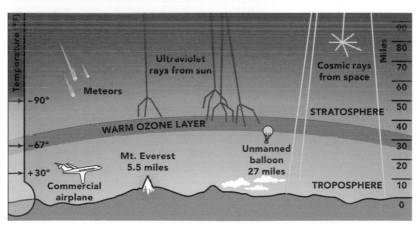

THE WEIGHT of the Earth's atmosphere is tremendous: 5,000,000,000,000,000 (5 quadrillion) tons. The pressure of the air against the Earth (at sea level) is about 15 pounds per square inch. Because the surface area of the average person is 2,700 square inches, the air pressure against a human body is about 20 tons. The reason that the body does not collapse is that the atmospheric pressure outside of the body is counteracted by an equal amount of pressure from within. As a matter of fact, if the pressure outside the body were eliminated (as in outer space), the skin and tissue would rapidly swell as water in the body begins to vaporize. (It is a myth that the human body would explode.) This is why airplanes designed to fly at high altitude have pressurized cabins. This also is why astronauts and some military pilots wear pressure suits.

MERCURY IS USED in liquid barometers because it is such a heavy liquid; it weighs 13.6 times as much as water. Water could be used in place of mercury, but the column of water in such a barometer would have to be 34 feet tall (instead of 2.5 feet tall in the case of a mercurial barometer). The observer would have to climb a ladder to read the atmospheric pressure.

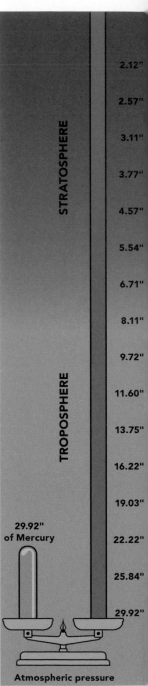

STRATOSPHERE

TROPOSPHERE

2.12"
2.57"
3.11"
3.77"
4.57"
5.54"
6.71"
8.11"
9.72"
11.60"
13.75"
16.22"
19.03"
22.22"
25.84"
29.92"

29.92"
of Mercury

Atmospheric pressure

Altitude	Temperature
60,000 ft	−70°F
56,000 ft	−70°F
52,000 ft	−70°F
48,000 ft	−70°F
44,000 ft	−70°F
40,000 ft	−70°F
36,000 ft	−69°F
32,000 ft	−55°F
28,000 ft	−41°F
24,000 ft	−27°F
20,000 ft	−12°F
16,000 ft	2°F
12,000 ft	16°F
8,000 ft	31°F
4,000 ft	45°F
Sea Level	59°F

ATMOSPHERIC PRESSURE can be measured with a mercurial barometer, which consists of a calibrated glass tube sealed at one end and filled with liquid mercury. The open end is immersed in a container of mercury. At sea level, air pressing down on the mercury in the container keeps the mercury in the tube at a height of 29.92 inches. This is known as standard sea-level pressure.

As we fly higher in the atmosphere, the air becomes thinner (less dense), the pressure decreases, and the column of mercury in a barometer falls. At 18,000 feet, atmospheric pressure is only half as great (14.94 inches of mercury) as at sea level. The air pressure at 40,000 feet is only 5.54 inches. At the upper limits of the atmosphere, the air is extremely thin and has practically no pressure at all.

THE TEMPERATURE of the air at sea level over the Earth averages 59°F (15°C). As altitude increases, temperature decreases at the rate of 3.5°F (2°C) per 1,000 feet until it reaches about −70°F (−57°C) at 7 miles above the Earth. This marks the boundary between the lowest layer of the atmosphere, the *troposphere*, and the second layer, the *stratosphere*, which extends from 7 to 50 miles above the Earth. The temperature throughout the stratosphere remains relatively constant and does not decrease with altitude. The temperature in outer space is absolute zero, or −459°F (−273°C). The vast majority of light airplanes fly in the troposphere, and this is where most weather occurs.

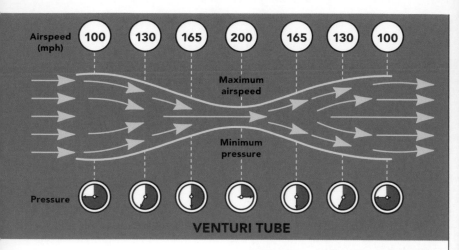

VENTURI TUBE

AIRSPEED AND AIR PRESSURE are related in a way that is crucial to flight. This relationship is illustrated by the flow of air through a *Venturi tube.* As air flows through the constricted throat at the center of the tube, it speeds up in the same way that water does when it flows through the nozzle of a garden hose. As the air leaves the constricted throat of the Venturi tube, its speed decreases.

When air flows past a surface, it creates a low-pressure area, or partial vacuum, causing the air to exert a suction effect against the surface. The greater the airspeed, the lower will be the pressure. As air flows through a Venturi tube, its speed increases and its pressure decreases as the tube becomes narrower. The greatest speed and the least air pressure occur where the tube is narrowest. As the tube widens again, the airspeed decreases, and the air pressure increases. This inverse relationship between airspeed and air pressure is a key principle responsible for flight.

A BASIC PRINCIPLE OF FLIGHT can be demonstrated by the flow of water through a garden hose. **(A)** If the hose has no nozzle, water flows out the end at the same speed as it flows through the length of the hose. **(B)** If you add a nozzle to the hose or place your thumb over part of the hose opening, the water comes out faster (and travels farther). It constricts the flow and increases the speed. In each case, the water travels faster because it is flowing through a smaller area. The increase in speed enables the same amount of water to flow from the hose in a given period of time. **(C)** If a wide funnel replaces the nozzle, the area of the hose opening is enlarged. The water flows more slowly and sloshes over the rim of the funnel.

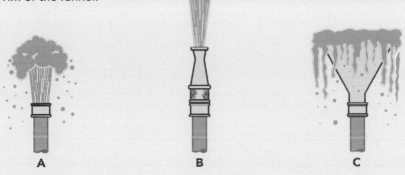

A   B   C

Air also is a fluid and behaves the same way as water. The effect of a constriction can be shown by blowing your breath against the palm of your hand. If you blow as hard as you can with your mouth wide open, the air leaves so slowly that you can barely feel it. But if you pucker your lips as though you were going to whistle and blow hard, the air comes out much faster. The air speeds up as it passes through the narrower opening formed by your lips.

If air is blown between two ping-pong balls suspended a few inches apart, the low pressure created by the air against the sides of the balls pulls them together. In the same way, a flow of water attracts a balloon, and a stream of air between two pieces of paper pulls them toward one another.

LIFT is the force that supports the weight of an airplane. For an airplane to maintain a given altitude, the (net) force of lift must be equal to the weight of the airplane. If lift exceeds weight, the airplane will climb (accelerate upward). If weight exceeds lift, the aircraft descends (accelerates downward).

The illustration below shows the flow of air about a wing in level flight. The upper surface is curved, or *cambered*. The bottom surface is relatively flat. Wing camber is very much like the bottom half of a Venturi tube (page 14). Air flowing immediately above the wing follows the curved contour just the way it does when

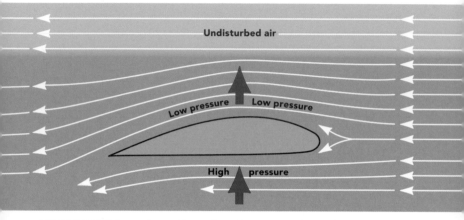

AIR FLOWING from the trailing edge of the wing is deflected somewhat downward. This action results in an opposite reaction that produces lift.

The lift created by a wing increases in proportion to the square of a wing's airspeed. This means that by doubling the airspeed of a wing (for example, from 100 to 200 mph), the lift produced is quadrupled (in this case, from 2,000 to 8,000 pounds). Increasing wing area also produces a proportionate increase in lift.

WING LIFT varies with air density. Assume that a given wing at sea level creates 2,000 pounds of lift. If that same wing is flown at high altitude (under the same conditions) where the air might be only half as dense, the wing would produce only 1,000 pounds of lift.

The wing loading of an airplane is a measure of how much lift each square foot of the wing develops (or how much aircraft weight it supports). For example, a wing with an area of 200 square feet that lifts an airplane weighing 2,000 pounds has a wing loading of 10 pounds per square foot.

flowing through the tube. The upper half of this airborne Venturi tube is the horizontal, undisturbed layer of air well above the wing. The air flowing immediately above the wing, therefore, is traveling through a constriction formed by the wing's curved upper surface. This causes the air to accelerate as it travels over the wing.

Increased airspeed over the wing lowers the air pressure above the wing. The air pressure beneath the wing remains relatively unchanged and is, therefore, greater than the pressure of air above the wing. This greater pressure below lifts the wing upward.

Lift is demonstrated by blowing air across the upper surface of a piece of paper, creating a low-pressure area. The higher pressure below the paper lifts it.

Both wings have the same wing area. The narrow wing is the most efficient, but the stubby wing can fly faster.

A high-speed airfoil   A high-lift airfoil

Wing shape is an important factor in aircraft design. The cross-sectional shape of a wing is called the airfoil.

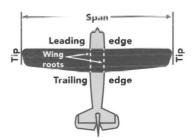

Span

Leading edge

Tip   Wing roots   Tip

Trailing edge

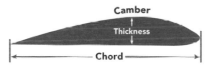

Camber

Thickness

Chord

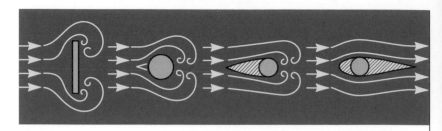

DRAG is the resistance of the air to an object moving through it. When you hold your hand out of a speeding automobile, you can feel the drag as a force pushing your hand rearward, especially when the hand is held flat to the direction of travel. Air resistance decreases if the palm is held parallel to the ground because less frontal area is exposed to the force of the resisting air.

An aircraft creates much drag because of its large size, so engineers try to design airplanes that create as little drag as possible. This technique is called streamlining.

Of all the objects shown above, the flat plate creates the most drag because it disturbs the flow of air the most. The more streamlined the object, the less drag it produces.

THE SPEED at which an object travels through the air affects drag. The faster an object travels, the more drag it creates. In fact, the increase in drag is proportional to the square of the airspeed. This means that doubling the speed quadruples the drag. Thus, an airplane that creates 500 pounds of drag force at 100 mph creates 2,000 pounds at 200 mph. The less drag an airplane creates, the faster it can fly.

Retractable landing gear eliminates the drag during flight caused by wheels and struts.

THRUST is the force created with engine power to overcome drag. When thrust equals drag, an airplane is in equilibrium and maintains a constant airspeed. If thrust is increased by adding power, the airplane accelerates because thrust is greater than drag. If thrust is reduced by reducing power, drag will be greater than thrust. The resisting force will be greater than the forward thrust, so the aircraft slows down. Because speed is a factor producing drag, an airplane can establish a balance between drag and thrust to maintain either a relatively high, intermediate, or low airspeed.

AN ENGINE can produce thrust by the reaction of a jet (page 66) or by turning a propeller. The British refer to the propeller as an *air screw* because thrust is seemingly created by a propeller as it advances through the air the way a wood screw advances into a block of wood. More accurately, a propeller hurls a great deal of air rearward. This rearward action causes the forward reaction called thrust.

A rotating propeller creates horizontal lift to pull the airplane forward.

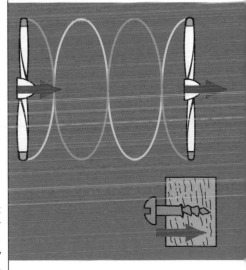

A propeller screws through the air the way a wood screw advances into a block of wood.

AIRCRAFT DESIGN varies considerably from one type to the next. This is because each type of aircraft is designed to fulfill a specific purpose. Some are designed to fly fast, while others are intended to carry heavy loads. Some are built for landing on rough terrain; others are not. Some are built to maximize comfort and stability, while others are designed to sell at a low price. Aircraft built for military purposes are different than those intended to whisk passengers comfortably to distant destinations. The airplane designer uses some of the design concepts shown on the opposite page to suit the manufacturer's needs.

This twin-engine airplane is a low-wing monoplane with straight, rectangular, cantilever wings, retractable landing gear, tractor engines, and a T-tail.

Aircraft

Aircraft	
Airplanes	Single-engine, land Single-engine, sea Multi-engine, land Multi-engine, sea Amphibians
Gliders	Unpowered Powered
Lighter than Air	Airships Balloons
Powered Lift	Tiltrotor
Rotorcraft	Helicopters Gyroplanes
Light-Sport Aircraft (≤1,320 pounds)	Airplanes Gliders Powered parachutes Weight-shift control Lighter-than-air

WING PLACEMENT

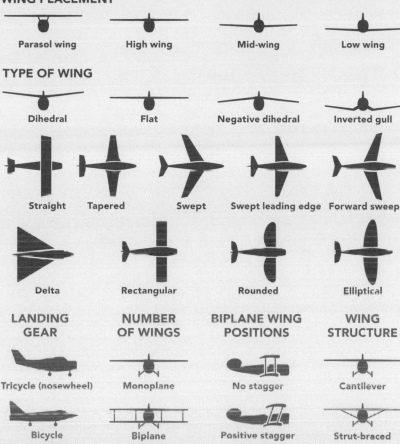

Parasol wing   High wing   Mid-wing   Low wing

TYPE OF WING

Dihedral   Flat   Negative dihedral   Inverted gull

Straight   Tapered   Swept   Swept leading edge   Forward sweep

Delta   Rectangular   Rounded   Elliptical

LANDING GEAR

Tricycle (nosewheel)

Bicycle

Conventional (tailwheel)

NUMBER OF WINGS

Monoplane

Biplane

Triplane

BIPLANE WING POSITIONS

No stagger

Positive stagger

Negative stagger

WING STRUCTURE

Cantilever

Strut-braced

THRUST METHOD

Pusher   Tractor

TAIL ARRANGEMENT

Conventional   T-tail   H-tail   Triple tail   V-tail   Cruciform

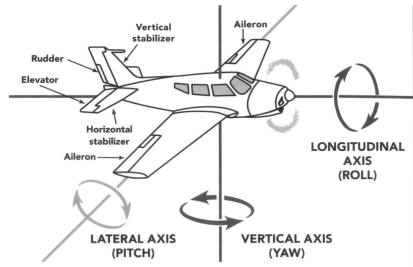

Vertical stabilizer

Aileron

Rudder

Elevator

Horizontal stabilizer

Aileron

LONGITUDINAL AXIS (ROLL)

LATERAL AXIS (PITCH)

VERTICAL AXIS (YAW)

FLIGHT CONTROLS are used to maintain or change the attitude of an airplane about its three axes—longitudinal, lateral, and vertical. The longitudinal axis is an imaginary line extending from the nose to the tail. Rotating an airplane about this axis is called *rolling* or *banking*. The lateral axis extends from one wingtip to the other. Movement about this axis is called *pitching*. Raising the nose increases the pitch attitude of the airplane, and lowering the nose decreases pitch. The vertical axis is perpendicular to the other two axes and passes through their intersection. Movement about this axis is called *yawing* or fishtailing.

Airplanes (and gliders) are equipped with three primary flight controls that change or maintain the attitude of the aircraft about these three axes. These controls are the *ailerons*, the *elevator*, and the *rudder*

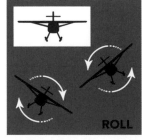

ROLL

PITCH

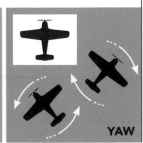

YAW

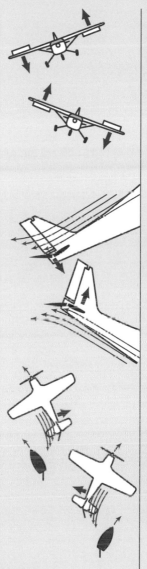

THE AILERONS, one near each wingtip, control roll (or bank). They are connected in such a way that they move opposite to one another. When the control wheel in the cockpit is turned left by the pilot, the left aileron rises, and the right aileron goes down. Air pressure against the top of the left aileron causes the left wing to go down (decreased lift). Air pressure against the bottom of the right aileron causes the right wing to rise (increased lift). These two actions (descending left wing and rising right wing) produce a roll to the left (a left bank). When the wheel is turned to the right, the aircraft banks to the right.

THE ELEVATOR, a horizontal control surface on the tail, controls pitch. When the pilot pulls back on the control wheel (or control stick), the elevator rises into the airstream. The force of air against its top surface pushes the tail down, causing the nose to rise. When the control wheel is pushed forward, the elevator deflects downward. This raises the tail and lowers the nose.

THE RUDDER, a vertical control surface on the tail, controls yaw. Although it acts like a boat's rudder in theory, it is seldom used the same way. Two rudder pedals are on the cockpit floor near the pilot's feet. Pushing the left pedal with the left foot deflects the rudder to the left. Air pressure against the rudder's left side forces the tail to move right and the nose of the airplane to yaw left. Pressing the right pedal with the right foot moves the tail left and the nose right.

A HIGH-WING AIRPLANE has parasol stability that dampens rolling. It tends to remain upright because its weight is concentrated beneath the wing.

LOW-WING AIRPLANES are made laterally stable by attaching the wings at an angle to the fuselage. This angle is called dihedral and dampens rolling.

STABLE

NEUTRAL

UNSTABLE

STABILITY is the property that causes an aircraft to return (by itself) to its original attitude after its balance has been disturbed. A rounded cone *(lower left)* is stable because it will revert to its original position if tipped. A cone resting on its tip is unstable; once the cone falls, it cannot raise itself to its original upright position. A ball is neutrally stable; it remains in any position in which it is placed.

An arrow shot through the air is stable because of its feathers. Without them, the arrow would be an unstable stick that would wallow and tumble through the air. On airplanes, parts called *stabilizers* serve a similar function as tail features. The fixed surface to which the rudder is attached is the *vertical stabilizer* (page 22). It provides directional stability by dampening yaw movements. The fixed surface to which the elevator is attached is the *horizontal stabilizer*. It dampens pitch movements and provides longitudinal stability.

TRIMMING an airplane is adjusting the flight controls so that the airplane remains in the same attitude (no rolling, pitching, or yawing) without further help from the pilot. For example, to raise the nose (as when establishing a climb) and keep it raised, the pilot must apply continuous back pressure on the control wheel. This effort can be relieved by using the trim tab on the trailing edge of the elevator. The position of the tab is adjusted in the cockpit by turning the trim wheel or crank. Unlike an elevator, a trim tab remains in whatever position it is set.

If the pilot wants the aircraft to remain in a nose high attitude, he applies nose-up trim. The small tab deflects downward into the airstream. The force of air pushing against the tab causes the elevator to deflect upward, which in turn makes the nose go up and stay up.

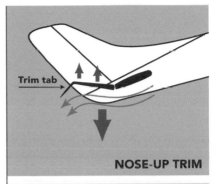

NOSE-UP TRIM

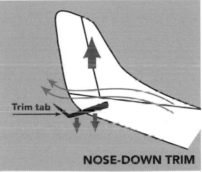

NOSE-DOWN TRIM

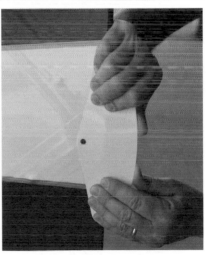

If a pilot has to apply continuous rudder pressure to prevent a yaw, the pilot can eliminate this tiring procedure in flight by adjusting a hinged trim tab on the rudder *(left)*. Rudder trim tabs on some small aircraft *(right)* can be adjusted (bent by hand) only on the ground to correct a yaw tendency detected during an earlier flight.

RELATIVE WIND is the wind created by movement of an object through the air. Relative wind always "blows" opposite to the direction of travel and at the same speed. The tremendous forces needed to provide aircraft lift and control are produced by the relative wind created by the airplane's motion through the air. Determining the direction from which the relative wind is blowing is not as easy when flying as when riding a bicycle. This is because an airplane often points in one direction while actually traveling in another. Also, a pilot in a closed cockpit cannot feel the relative wind.

The relative wind opposes a bicycle rider pedaling up, across, and down a hill at each point along the way. The faster the bicycle travels, the stronger the relative wind becomes. When the rider stops, the relative wind disappears.

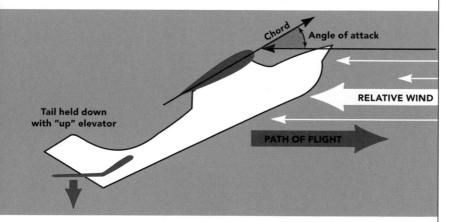

The aircraft above is pointed upward as if in a climb, but it is actually maintaining a constant altitude (a maneuver called slow flight). The relative wind is opposite to the horizontal flight path. It is not opposite to the direction in which the airplane is pointing.

ANGLE OF ATTACK is the angle formed by the relative wind and a wing's chord. It determines how much lift is created at a given airspeed. The wing *(below)* with the larger angle of attack produces the most lift.

LIFT VS. ANGLE OF ATTACK

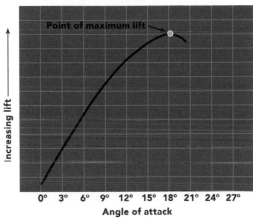

Point of maximum lift

Increasing lift

0° 3° 6° 9° 12° 15° 18° 21° 24° 27°
Angle of attack

Air flowing over the wing with the large angle of attack travels through a narrower constriction (page 16) than air flowing over the other wing. The air travels faster than when at a small angle of attack (for a given aircraft airspeed), decreasing pressure above the wing and increasing lift.

Additional lift is provided by air deflected from the bottom of the wing. This is similar to the lift created by a kite. Air striking the bottom of the wing (or kite) pushes against the surface and causes it to rise.

A pilot controls the wing's angle of attack with the elevator. Applying back pressure to the control wheel raises the elevator. This raises the nose and increases the wing's angle of attack. Pushing the control wheel forward lowers the nose and decreases the angle of attack.

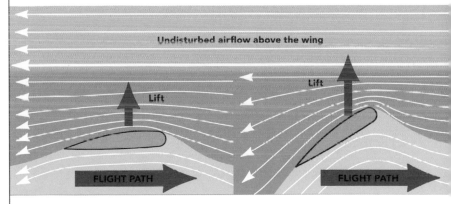

Undisturbed airflow above the wing

Lift

Lift

FLIGHT PATH

FLIGHT PATH

INCREASING the angle of attack increases aircraft drag because the wing is no longer streamlined with the relative wind. When the angle of attack is decreased, drag decreases, resulting in higher airspeed. In effect, the elevator (which directly controls angle of attack) helps to determine aircraft speed.

SMOOTH AIRFLOW over the wing is necessary for a wing to develop lift. When the pilot excessively increases the wing's angle of attack with up elevator, the air cannot flow smoothly over the wing. Instead, it breaks up into turbulent eddies, destroying the low-pressure region above the wing. This is a stall. Lift is lost and the airplane descends. Stall recovery requires 100–300 feet of altitude loss.

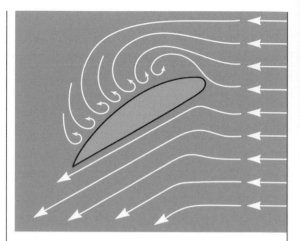

A STALL is the loss of lift that occurs when a wing is flown at too large an angle of attack. The air cannot change direction sharply enough to follow the contour of the wing's upper surface. Instead, the air burbles over the wing. Lift is lost, and the wing can no longer support the aircraft.

The speed at which an airplane stalls depends on several factors. A heavily loaded airplane stalls at a higher speed than one that is lightly loaded. Stalling speed is higher during a turn than when the wings are level. The stalling speed typically is lower with the engine delivering power than when it is idling (no power).

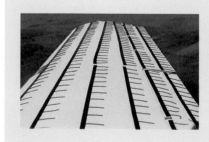

The photographs above help to visualize a stall. Small strands of yarn are taped along the upper surface of the wing. The wing on the left is in climbing flight; the smooth airflow over the wing blows the yarn straight back. The wing on the right is in a stalled condition. The burbling air over the wing causes the strands to wriggle and squirm unevenly.

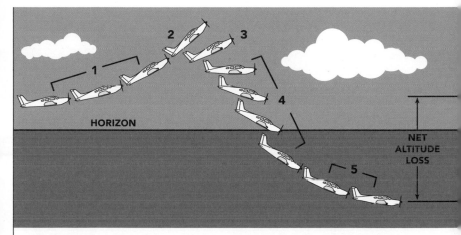

HORIZON

NET ALTITUDE LOSS

DETECTING A STALL before it occurs, even without warning devices, is something pilots learn to do by feel, sound, and aircraft performance. Stalls generally, but not always, occur at low speeds. The controls are not as effective as they are at higher speeds, and they can feel mushy and less responsive. Also, as the airspeed gets lower, the sound of the relative wind against the windshield and cabin becomes quieter. The final warning comes from the airplane itself. As air burbles across the wing, a light shudder (vibration) usually can be felt throughout the aircraft.

Almost all airplanes have a stall-warning indicator. It typically is a blowing horn or flashing red light on the instrument panel (or both) that warns the pilot when the aircraft is close to stalling. Larger airplanes have stick shakers that vibrate the control wheel to warn of an impending stall. Some airplanes even have stick pushers that automatically initiate the process of stall recovery.

RECOVERY from a stall requires eliminating the cause of the stall—an excessive angle of attack. When the wing stalls and loses lift, the aircraft begins to yield to the unrelenting pull of gravity. Stalls are only dangerous near the ground, where sufficient altitude might not be available to execute recovery. Student pilots practice stalls and stall recovery at a safe altitude. (It is not as frightening as it might sound.)

(1) A stall is entered by applying back pressure to the control wheel (up-elevator), which increases the wing's angle of attack. (2) When the angle of attack becomes excessive, the air burbles over the wing, and the pilot might feel a mild buffeting of the aircraft. (3) To recover, the pilot releases the back pressure on the control wheel and lowers the nose. (4) When a safe flying speed has been restored, the pilot applies gentle back pressure on the control wheel and levels off or enters a climb. (5) The pilot applies full throttle during stall recovery to minimize altitude loss.

FLAPS are movable portions of a wing's trailing edge. They look like ailerons but are nearer to the fuselage. Flaps help solve the designer's dilemma—how to produce a wing that flies well at both high and low speeds. High speed reduces travel time, and low speed for takeoff and landing eliminates the need for excessively long runways.

Two aircraft with flaps extended.

When retracted (up), flaps are an integral part of the high-speed wing. When extended (down), they increase the overall camber (curvature) of the wing, enabling it to produce more lift at lower speeds. Some flaps, when lowered, also increase wing area.

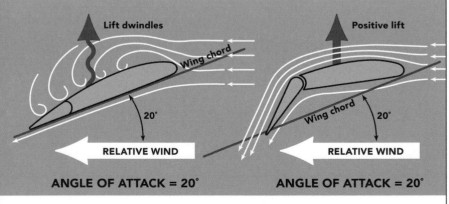

When flown at a 20° angle of attack, the wing with flaps retracted (left) stalls. With the flaps extended (right), the wing can produce lift at the same angle of attack.

WING PERFORMANCE can be varied by the use of flaps. To increase the wing's lift for takeoff, a pilot lowers the flaps partially. They are not extended fully because they would create too much drag, and this would hinder acceleration and initial climb performance. After takeoff when the flaps are no longer needed, they are retracted and remain so during cruise flight. Otherwise, they would inhibit high-speed performance.

During a landing approach, the pilot needs to lose altitude. If the pilot accomplished this by diving at the runway, airspeed would increase, and excess runway length (which might not be available) would be required to land and roll to a stop. In this case, the drag created by lowering flaps becomes an advantage. Extending the flaps all the way helps to prevent airspeed from increasing during a descent.

SLOTS also are useful at low speeds. At large angles of attack, air from beneath the wing flows through a slot and over the rear portion of the wing, reducing the speed at which a stall would occur. The slot is a permanent gap in the wing.

LEADING-EDGE FLAPS operate on the principle of trailing-edge flaps: they increase both wing camber and wing area. Leading-edge flaps are retracted during cruise flight.

SLATS combine the advantages of leading-edge flaps and slots. In cruise flight, the slat is moved to fit flush against the wing, which closes the slot.

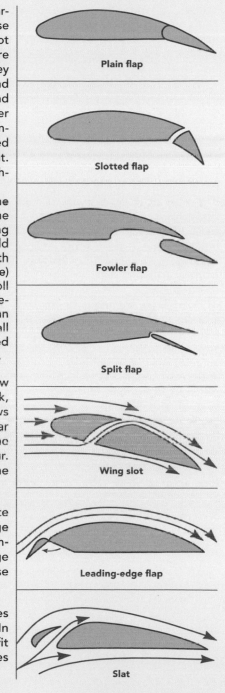

Plain flap

Slotted flap

Fowler flap

Split flap

Wing slot

Leading-edge flap

Slat

TURNS are confusing to most non-pilots, who assume that if a rudder turns a boat, it also turns an airplane. This is incorrect; a rudder does not turn an airplane.

In straight-and-level flight **(A)**, the lift of the wing is perpendicular to the wing; it acts vertically, directly opposing the force of gravity. The relationship of lift to a wing does not change when the airplane is banked. The aircraft in **(B)** is in a 45-degree bank, yet the lift is still (and always is) perpendicular to the wing. If an airplane is rolled into a 90-degree bank **(C)**, all lift is horizontal, or inward. There is no upward lift to oppose gravity, and thus the airplane is unable to maintain altitude and descends.

Turning an airplane is similar to whirling a ball in a circle at the end of a string *(next page)*. The force of the string pulling on the ball acts inward to make the ball travel in a curved path (turn) and also acts upward to prevent the ball from falling to the ground. The lift of the wing is just like the string. Both represent identical forces. The wing's lift whirls the plane in a circle just the way the string makes the ball travel in a circle.

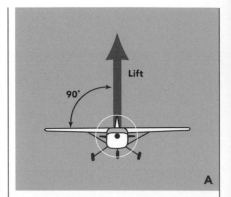

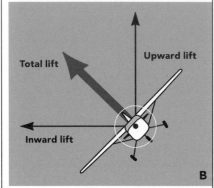

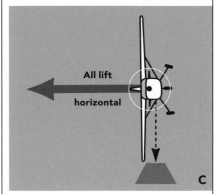

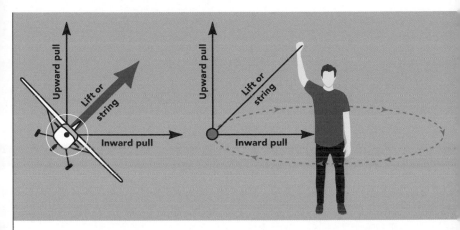

WHEN AN AIRPLANE BANKS, the force of lift acts toward one side of the aircraft; it pulls upward and inward on the airplane. The upward pull of lift opposes gravity. The inward pull of lift causes the airplane to turn in the direction of bank. The steeper an airplane is banked, the greater will be its rate of turn. For example, an airplane flying at 100 mph in a 20-degree bank makes a complete circle (a 360-degree turn) in 79 seconds. If the bank angle is doubled (40 degrees), the time required is only 34 seconds. If the bank angle is tripled (60 degrees), the time required is only 17 seconds.

AIRSPEED also affects rate of turn. The faster an airplane flies, the slower it turns at a given bank angle; the lower the airspeed, the more rapid is the turn rate. For example, an airplane flying at 100 mph in a 45-degree bank needs 29 seconds to fly in a circle. If airspeed is increased to 150 mph (while at the same bank angle), the airplane makes a bigger circle and 43 seconds are required.

CHAPTER 3
AIRCRAFT VARIETY

MULTI-ENGINE AIRCRAFT • SEAPLANES • SKIPLANES • GLIDERS • BALLOONS
AIRSHIPS • HELICOPTERS • POWERED-LIFT AIRCRAFT • AIRLINERS • MILITARY AIRCRAFT
UNMANNED AERIAL VEHICLES • LIGHT-SPORT AIRCRAFT • ULTRALIGHT AIRCRAFT
ANTIQUE AIRCRAFT • HOMEBUILT/AMATEUR-BUILT AIRCRAFT

TWIN-ENGINE AIRPLANES can fly safely with only one engine operating. Most three-engine and all four-engine airplanes can do the same with two failed engines. It is even possible for some lightly loaded four-engine airplanes to maintain a low altitude and slow airspeed with only one engine operating. The procedures required to control a conventional twin-engine airplane during and following an engine failure represent the most significant difference between flying such an airplane and flying a single-engine airplane.

The failure of two or more engines at the same time is extremely unlikely. Each engine operates independently and has its own set of controls and systems.

A FAILED LEFT ENGINE is shown in this illustration. The thrust produced by the right engine coupled with the drag (air resistance) of the left engine causes the airplane to yaw to the left. The pilot must apply right rudder-pedal pressure to prevent yawing and keep the airplane pointed straight ahead. A failed right engine creates a yaw to the right that must be countered with left rudder-pedal pressure.

The yaw created by an engine failure is similar to the yaw of a rowboat when one oar is used to pull and the other is allowed to simply drag in the water.

LEFT YAW

THRUST

DRAG

YAW

This oar pulling

This oar dragging

Right rudder required to stop yaw

WHEN AN ENGINE FAILS, its propeller continues to turn like a windmill. This creates drag and hampers the airplane's already handicapped performance. Most of this drag is eliminated by *feathering* (twisting) the propeller blades so that they are aligned parallel to the relative wind and slice through the air *(left)*. The propeller then stops windmilling (ceases its spin), and this could eliminate further engine damage.

Feathering the propeller blades eliminates the drag created by a windmilling propeller.

AT LOW AIRSPEEDS, the rudder is not as effective as at high airspeeds; there is less air flowing past it. During a steep climb when airspeed is low, the rudder force may not be sufficiently effective to counteract a yaw caused by an engine failure. To prevent the undesirable yaw at such a time, the pilot has two choices: lower the nose and accelerate to a speed where the rudder becomes more effective, or reduce the amount of power produced by the operative engine (if practical), which reduces the force creating the yaw.

A PROBLEM arising at the instant of engine failure is for the pilot to quickly determine which engine failed. This is not as easy as it sounds. One way is to survey the engine power instruments. Another is to apply whatever rudder pressure is required to keep the airplane pointed straight ahead. The foot not applying rudder pressure is on the same side as the dead engine. In other words, "dead foot, dead engine."

A CENTERLINE-THRUST aircraft is a twin-engine airplane with both engines mounted on the airplane's longitudinal centerline. An engine failure creates no undesirable yaw in this type of aircraft, which will continue to fly straight ahead. The power loss, however, will result in a reduction in the airplane's ability to climb, its service ceiling, and its cruise speed.

This twin-engine aircraft is powered by two wing-mounted reciprocating (piston) engines.

This Ford Trimotor airplane has one engine on each wing and one on the nose.

This twin-engine, centerline-thrust airplane has a tractor engine in front and a pusher engine in back.

FLOATPLANES AND FLYING BOATS are the two types of seaplanes. The floatplane *(above)* is generally a modified landplane on which floats replace wheels and landing gear. The flying boat is specifically designed for operating on water, with a hull shaped like that of a boat. A small float (or pontoon) on each wing prevents the wings from striking the water and possibly capsizing the airplane. Floats and hulls each contain several watertight compartments designed to prevent a leak in one compartment from flooding the entire float or hull and causing the airplane to sink.

SEAPLANES take off and land on water. They fly more slowly than comparable landplanes because of the drag (air resistance) created by flotation hulls. These hulls also add considerable weight.

Maneuvering on water requires special techniques because a seaplane has no brakes. An untethered seaplane can be at the mercy of the wind and the movement of the water. A light breeze or water current can drift the aircraft into an obstacle.

When on the water, a seaplane behaves like an oversized weather vane that turns into the wind. A pilot must sail a seaplane almost like a sailor does a boat. The pilot controls the seaplane's path on the water by skillful use of engine power and small underwater rudders.

Even though a seaplane does not have brakes, it can often land in a shorter distance than a comparable landplane because a fast-moving object in the water creates considerable drag (water resistance). A landing seaplane slows quickly. Takeoff distances in water are generally longer for the same reason.

When a seaplane reaches takeoff speed, the water flowing under the curved hulls creates reduced pressure. This is like lift working in the opposite direction; the water holds the airplane down. The pilot can overcome this by abruptly applying back-pressure on the control wheel, which "jerks" the airplane from the water.

LANDING on smooth, glassy water is more difficult than landing on rippled or wavy water. This is because judging height above a smooth, reflective surface is deceptive; depth perception is distorted.

AN AMPHIBIAN can be either a flying boat or a floatplane that is equipped with retractable wheels so that it can land on both land and water.

Amphibian pilots must be especially careful during a landing approach to ensure that the wheels are positioned properly. A touchdown in the water with the wheels extended or on land with the wheels retracted can cause structural damage to the aircraft and possible injury to those inside.

SKIPLANES can land on snow. Like seaplanes, they do not have brakes. Short-distance landings are made by landing uphill, but the pilot must turn the skiplane at an angle to the slope before coming to a stop. Otherwise, the aircraft could ski backward down the slope. Takeoffs are made downhill (if possible).

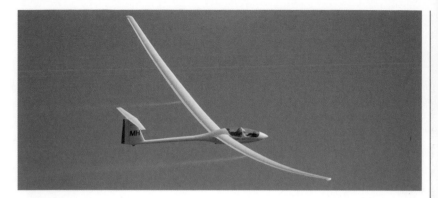

GLIDERS are to the sky as sailboats are to the sea. This is why they are also called sailplanes. By flying in rising air, glider pilots can climb to great heights, soar long distances, and remain aloft for many hours. World gliding records include a climb to 76,124 feet above sea level (higher than all jetliners can fly) and a flight distance of 1,869 statute miles.[1]

A glider is an unpowered, heavier-than-air aircraft that climbs for the same reason that ashes (also heavier than air) rise from a fire. In still air, a glider might descend at 200 feet per minute. But if the air in which it is flying rises at the same rate, the glider maintains a constant altitude. If the air rises more rapidly, the glider will also rise and gain altitude.

Gliders have the same basic flight controls as airplanes and are flown in much the same manner. Because a glider does not have an engine, it must be towed aloft. Airplane tows are best because the glider can be towed to where good soaring conditions exist. Automobiles and winches can launch a glider to only about 1,200 feet above the airport.

Some gliders are equipped with small engines and are called motor-gliders or self-launching sailplanes. The pilot takes off in the same manner as in an airplane, flies to where good soaring conditions exist, shuts down the engine, and soars in the manner of a glider pilot. If soaring conditions weaken, the pilot can restart the engine and fly somewhere else.

This motorglider has an electric motor used for self-launching (taking off). It is shut down during flight and retracted into the top of the fuselage when the aircraft is used as a sailplane (glider) for soaring.

There are **THREE TYPES OF SOARING**: thermal soaring, ridge soaring, and wave soaring. Each is defined by the manner in which air is caused to rise.

THERMAL SOARING is done in a thermal, a bubble of air that has been heated by the ground and rises because it is warmer than the surrounding air. If the thermal is large enough and warm enough, it can lift a glider to higher altitudes. As the thermal rises, it cools. If it contains sufficient moisture, this cooling can cause a cumulus cloud to form. A cumulus cloud is a visual sign of rising air. Long-distance flights can be made by flying from one thermal to the next.

RIDGE SOARING is done in air that is deflected upward when wind blows against the slope of a hill or mountain. Under the proper conditions of wind speed, wind direction, and slope steepness, a glider can soar back and forth along the windward side of a ridge for many hours at a time. The pilot must avoid flying on the leeward or downwind side of the ridge because of the downdrafts (sinking currents) that are found there.

WAVE SOARING is done on mountain waves. Such waves can form when a strong wind (more than 25 mph) blows over the ridges of high, steep mountains. Good soaring conditions (rising air) are found on the windward sides of wave crests. Strong downdrafts are found on the opposite sides. Lens-shaped lenticular clouds indicate the location of a wave crest. At such altitudes, pilots usually need to use supplemental oxygen.

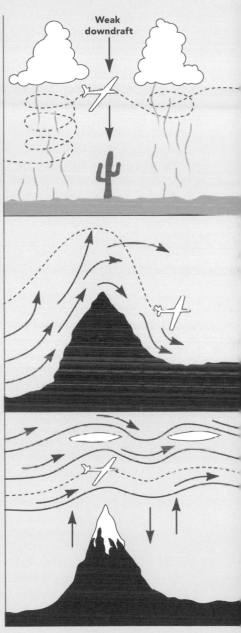

Weak downdraft

FREE BALLOONS fly because they are buoyant. When filled with hot air or helium, they are literally lighter than air. They are also the oldest successful man-carrying technology.

The first aircraft to carry passengers was a hot-air balloon. In 1783, the Montgolfier brothers of France ignited a fire beneath their aerostat, filled it with hot air, and sent it aloft carrying a sheep, a rooster, and a duck. One purpose of the experiment was to determine if animals (and, therefore, people) could survive flight. (Skeptics thought that flying would be a fatal experience.) The first manned flight took place two months later.

The basket in which pilot and passengers are carried is called a *gondola*. The entire aircraft is referred to as a *balloon* and the lifting portion is called the *envelope*.

A balloon pilot, also called an aeronaut, cannot control a balloon's direction of flight. The aircraft is unpowered and is free to drift with the wind, explaining why such aircraft are called free balloons. Because a balloon cannot fly against the wind, the pilot and passengers do not feel a breeze.

If a balloon pilot dislikes the direction in which the wind is blowing the aircraft, the only two choices are to change altitude and hopefully find wind blowing in a more desirable direction or to land. A ground crew often follows in a car to assist the pilot in securing the balloon after landing.

Balloons tied to the ground and allowed only to rise to a limited height are called tethered balloons.

HOT-AIR BALLOONS gain altitude when the pilot operates a propane-burning heater to increase the temperature of the air in the envelope. The warmer the air in the envelope, the greater is the rate of climb. To descend, air in the envelope is allowed to cool. The descent rate can be increased by allowing some of the air in the envelope to escape through a vent controlled by the pilot. The pilot maintains altitude by operating the burner for approximately 5–10 seconds per minute.

When operating, the burner is noisy, but riding in a balloon the rest of the time is peaceful and serene. Some balloons are equipped with turning vents that allow the pilot to pivot the balloon about its vertical axis to align the gondola for landing. The envelope usually is made of lightweight and strong synthetic fabric such as ripstop nylon or Dacron.

GAS BALLOONING is not as popular as hot-air ballooning because filling an envelope with helium or hydrogen is more expensive than the propane used to generate hot air. Hydrogen is lighter than helium and provides greater lifting, but it is flammable and care must be taken not to expose it to sparks, lit cigarettes, electronic devices, and other forbidden items.

Gas balloons tend to rise to their *equilibrium altitude* and stay there. Altitude is increased by jettisoning ballast (usually water or sand) carried aboard the balloon. A descent is made by opening a valve at the top of the envelope and releasing some of the lifting gas. Landing should be made while the pilot still has sufficient ballast aboard the balloon to execute a missed approach. After all ballast has been jettisoned, the pilot no longer has the ability to reduce descent rate or to climb.

AIRSHIPS are sausage-shaped, lighter-than-air aircraft that are powered through the air by one or more engines. They have flight controls that enable the pilot to turn the airship right and left and to pitch it nose up and nose down. Because airships can be steered or directed through the air, they also are known as dirigibles.

Like balloons, airships are buoyant because they are filled with a large volume of helium. Hydrogen is lighter than helium and has greater lifting power, but it is flammable and has not been used in airships since the German airship *Hindenburg* was destroyed by fire while approaching to land at Lakehurst, New Jersey, in 1937.

At sea level, air and helium weigh 81 and 11 pounds per 1,000 cubic feet, respectively. This means that each 1,000 cubic feet of helium can lift 70 pounds of airship weight. An airship weighing 12,000 pounds (including fuel, crew, and passengers) requires more than 170,000 cubic feet of helium. This explains why airships are usually so large.

This helium-filled Model GZ-20 blimp has a cruise speed of 30 knots and a maximum allowable airspeed of 43 knots.

The pilot and passengers are carried in a gondola that rests on a single landing-gear wheel. One of this blimp's two pusher engines can be seen on the left, aft area of the gondola.

There are two types of airships: rigid and non-rigid. The rigid airship (Zeppelin) consists of a skeletal framework upon which the outer covering is attached. The non-rigid airship (blimp) is simply a sealed bag. Its shape is maintained by the pressure of the lifting gas inside for the same reason that a child's balloon maintains its shape.

Airships can be flown in any direction. They are not entirely at the mercy of the wind, as are balloons. However, because airships are so large and create so much drag, they are not very fast and typically cannot fly more than 30–50 mph.

The pilot and passengers ride in a compartment called a gondola attached to the underside of the airship. Airships are equipped with rudders and elevators but do not have ailerons and cannot be made to bank. They fly so slowly that the effects of skidding turns (using rudder only) present no problems. Because airships are like huge weather vanes, they cannot land in a crosswind; they must be landed exactly into the wind.

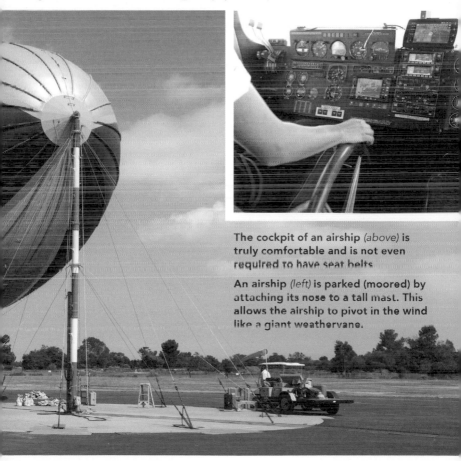

The cockpit of an airship (above) is truly comfortable and is not even required to have seat belts.

An airship (left) is parked (moored) by attaching its nose to a tall mast. This allows the airship to pivot in the wind like a giant weathervane.

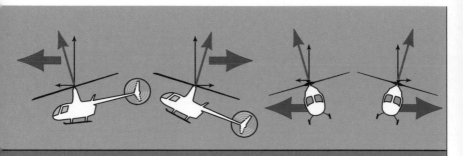

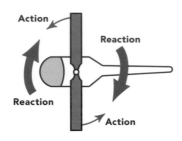

WITHOUT TAIL ROTOR

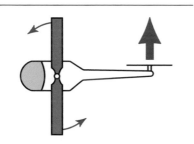

WITH TAIL ROTOR

When viewed from above, the rotor blades usually rotate counterclockwise. This produces a reaction—a torque that attempts to rotate the helicopter in a clockwise direction. A small tail rotor produces sideways "lift" that counteracts this turning force and enables the helicopter to fly straight ahead.

HELICOPTERS create lift using engine-driven rotor blades that rotate about the vertical axis of the aircraft. These blades are long, narrow wings that generate lift from the strong relative wind created as the blades revolve rapidly through the air. This allows a helicopter to hover over a spot. A helicopter can fly without forward motion.

The lift created by the rotor blades acts perpendicular to their plane of rotation. The pilot uses the control stick, called the cyclic control, to tilt the plane of rotor rotation (also called the rotor disc). When the pilot pulls back on the cyclic, the plane of rotation tilts aft. As a result, the force of lift tilts aft *(see above)*, and the helicopter flies backward. By pushing forward on the cyclic, the lift generated by the rotor disc tilts forward and the helicopter moves forward.

Moving the cyclic control to the left tilts the rotor disc to the left. The lift generated by the rotor blades tilts left, and this causes the helicopter to bank in that direction. Similarly, moving the cyclic control to the right causes the helicopter to bank to the right.

ADDITIONAL LIFT is obtained by raising the collective-pitch control that is located to the pilot's left. This increases the angle of attack of all rotor blades (collectively) and causes the helicopter to rise. Lowering the collective control causes the aircraft to descend. A motorcycle-style throttle on the end of the collective-pitch control adjusts engine power.

HELICOPTER ROTOR BLADES revolve slowly compared to propellers, but the blade tip speeds are fast at 500–700 mph. This is because the blades are so long. If the blades rotated faster, the tips would reach the speed of sound, lose effectiveness, and vibrate dangerously. Propellers also are limited by the speed of sound, but they rotate faster than rotor blades because they are shorter.

TWO FOOT PEDALS in a helicopter control yaw, the left–right movement of the nose. Pushing the left pedal increases the angle of attack of the tail blades. This increases the force created by the tail rotor, which moves the helicopter's tail to the right and nose to the left. Pushing the right pedal has the opposite effect and causes a yaw to the right.

GYROPLANES (autogyros) differ from helicopters in that their rotors are not powered. Forward speed is produced by an engine-propeller combination (like an airplane). The relative wind created by the gyroplane's movement through the air rotates the free-wheeling rotor blades like a windmill. This rotation enables the rotor blades to create lift. Gyroplanes can fly slowly and land in very short distances, but they cannot hover over a spot the way helicopters can. A tail rotor is not needed because unpowered rotors do not create torque.

POWERED-LIFT AIRCRAFT are heavier-than-air aircraft that can take off and land vertically but do not rely on rotors for lift during horizontal flight.

The Harrier *(above)* **takes off vertically by pointing its nozzles downward and lifting off in the fashion of a rocket ship.**

An exhaust nozzle on a Jump Jet *(inset)***. Once safely above the ground, the pilot gradually repositions the nozzles to point aft, and the aircraft accelerates into forward flight. When engine exhaust is directed rearward, all lift is provided by the wings, and the aircraft operates like a conventional airplane.**

VECTORED THRUST technology is the operating principle of the first successful powered-lift aircraft, the British Hawker Siddeley Harrier, informally called the Jump Jet. The exhaust from the engine of a conventional jet airplane is directed aft through a tailpipe (an exhaust nozzle). This propels the airplane forward.

Although the Harrier has only one jet engine, it has four exhaust nozzles. Before takeoff, these nozzles are positioned by the pilot to point down (instead of rearward). In this manner, the jet exhaust is directed (or vectored) straight down. The Harrier rises slowly from the ground, and the pilot uses the control stick to adjust the nozzles and maintain control of the aircraft. Moving the stick fore and aft causes the aircraft to move forward and backward. Moving the stick left and right causes the aircraft to move sideways.

TILTROTOR technology is responsible for another type of powered-lift aircraft such as the Bell Boeing V-22 Osprey. This aircraft can take off and land like a helicopter and fly between locations like an airplane with huge propellers that are called proprotors. When on the ground, the Osprey is in *helicopter mode*. The engines on the wingtips are aligned vertically so that the proprotors act as helicopter rotors.

The counter-rotating proprotors do not generate net torque, so there is no need for a tail rotor as on conventional helicopters. Once off the ground, the pilot operates a thumb switch that slowly tilts the engines forward. The Osprey then begins to move forward. The more the engines are tilted horizontally, the faster the Osprey moves forward. When the engines are completely horizontal, the Osprey is in the *airplane mode*. The proprotors become gigantic propellers, and the wings provide needed lift. Returning to helicopter mode involves reducing power and gradually returning the engines to their vertical positions.

AN ENGINE FAILURE in an Osprey is not as dramatic as one in a conventional multi-engine airplane. The aircraft does not yaw toward the failed engine. The Osprey instead flies straight ahead. This is because the Osprey's engines are interconnected with a long shaft that automatically transfers half the power of the operating engine to the opposite proprotor. The only effect is a noticeable reduction of performance.

The engines of a tiltrotor aircraft are tilted up when the aircraft is used as a helicopter *(above)* and tilted forward when used as an airplane *(left)*.

AIRLINERS, by virtue of their weight, size, speed, and range, are extremely complex. Each different type of jetliner requires a crew specifically trained and certificated (licensed) for its intricate systems and procedures.

A typical cockpit (flight-deck) crew consists of two pilots—a captain and a first officer (co-pilot). Together they fly the airplane, communicate with air traffic control, navigate, cope with the challenges of weather, and operate the hydraulic, electrical, fuel, and environmental-control systems. There used to be a need for radio operators, navigators, and flight engineers, but these crewmembers were replaced by improved technology and automation.

During the late 1930s, the propeller-driven Douglas DC-3 was the world's most productive airliner. It was relatively uncomplicated compared to modern jetliners and carried 21 passengers at 185 mph on flights of up to 800 statute miles.

Today, a mammoth four-engine, widebody jetliner such as the Airbus A380 has a maximum-allowable gross weight of 1,268,000 pounds and can carry as many as 853 passengers for a distance of up to 8,500 nautical miles (9,775 statute miles) at a speed of Mach 0.85 (85 percent of the speed of sound).

Airbus A380.

Douglas DC-3.

Airbus A380 cockpit.

THE CONCORDE was at one time the world's fastest airliner. This supersonic transport (SST) flew at twice the speed of sound (Mach 2.0) and as high as 60,000 feet. Developed jointly by England and France, the Concorde was too costly to operate and is no longer in service.

MILITARY AIRCRAFT (or warplanes) are used to provide national security. They can be combat or non-combat aircraft and range from small observation airplanes and helicopters to supersonic fighters and long-range bombers. In 1962, the U.S. Department of Defense established a system that designates aircraft according to their basic mission. This system is used by all six branches of the U.S. military: Air Force, Navy, Army, Marine Corps, Coast Guard, and Space Force. In this way, we know, for example, that a B-52 must be a bomber.

U.S. Department of Defense Aircraft Designations

A	Attack (air to surface)
B	Bomber
C	Transport (cargo)
E	Equipped with special electronics
F	Fighter
K	Refueling tanker
L	Laser equipped
O	Observation
P	Maritime patrol
R	Reconnaissance
S	Anti-submarine warfare
T	Trainer
U	Utility
X	Special research

Additional designations are used to indicate the type of aircraft when other than a conventional airplane.

G	Glider
H	Helicopter
Q	Unmanned aerial vehicle
S	Spaceplane
V	Vertical takeoff and landing
Z	Lighter than air

Surplus military airplanes have been offered for sale to civilians since the end of War II. Called warbirds, these range from small liaison airplanes to propeller-driven bombers. Most common and relatively inexpensive are observation airplanes such as the **Cessna O-1 Bird Dog** *(bottom)* and training airplanes such as the **Beechcraft T-34 Mentor.** Civilians with greater resources can purchase World War II fighters and bombers such as the **North American P-51 Mustang** and the **B-25 Mitchell.**

UNMANNED AERIAL VEHICLES (UAVs) are commonly called drones, remotely piloted aircraft (RPAs), or uncrewed aircraft (UAs). An advantage of a drone is that pilots are not put at risk during combat missions. Also, provisions do not have to be made for a pilot or crew. There is no need for seats, windows, pilot controls, elaborate instrumentation, oxygen and pressurization systems, heating and air-conditioning systems, ejection and survival equipment, and so forth. As a result, a UAV is lighter, arguably less complex, and more efficient than a comparable airplane designed to carry a pilot or crew.

Drones are controlled in one of two ways. The first is to program a flight plan into onboard computers and allow the aircraft to operate autonomously (by itself and with no additional or external control). The second and most common method of UAV control is to pilot the aircraft remotely via radio commands from a ground control station. A drone is regarded as recoverable and reusable.

Although the drone itself is called a UAV or RPA, the term *uncrewed aircraft system* (UAS) is used to include both the aircraft and the ground station used to control and guide the aircraft.

In a sense, a guided missile is a UAV but usually is not considered one because the vehicle itself is the weapon.

Smaller and less complex **CIVILIAN DRONES** are becoming increasingly popular and serve a multitude of roles, including surveillance of livestock, pipeline patrol, highway patrol, aerial surveying and photography, cinematography, journalism, law enforcement, search and rescue, and scientific research. The uses for drone technology are almost boundless.

A LIGHT-SPORT AIRCRAFT (LSA) in the United States is a small, low-performance aircraft that is less complex than larger, heavier aircraft and presumably is easier to fly. An aircraft with two seats (other than a helicopter or powered-lift aircraft) is considered an LSA as long as its takeoff weight is no more than 1,320 pounds and it has a maximum speed in level flight of 120 knots (138 mph) and a stall speed of no more than 45 knots (51 mph). It can have only one engine and must have a fixed-pitch propeller. An LSA may not be pressurized or have retractable landing gear (except for seaplanes and gliders that otherwise qualify as an LSA).

A WEIGHT-SHIFT CONTROL AIRPLANE is commonly called a trike because it has tricycle landing gear. It also has two seats, a small engine, and a triangular wing like those found on hang gliders. The pilot controls the aircraft by using body weight to assist in moving a control bar that is rigidly attached to the wing. The wing is mounted on a pivot above the aircraft. The pilot applies forces (fore and aft, and right and left) to the control bar. This moves the wing to produce desired changes in pitch and roll.

A POWERED PARACHUTE (or motorized parachute or paraplane) consists of a frame containing two seats and tricycle landing gear. A small engine is mounted on the rear of the frame, and the entire assembly is suspended from a parachute. Engine power is used to go up and down. The pilot steers by pulling on the right or left brake to change the shape of the parachute's sides and turn in the desired direction, just as skydivers do. It is a safe and inexpensive way to fly low and slow (25–35 mph).

One reason for the evolution of light-sport aircraft was to define a group of aircraft that could be flown with only a light-sport pilot certificate, a pilot's license that is not as difficult or expensive to obtain as the one required to fly larger, more complex, higher-performance aircraft.

There are certain restrictions, though. For example, a light-sport aircraft may not carry more than one passenger, fly at night, fly above 10,000 feet above sea level, fly when the visibility is less than 3 statute miles, fly without visual reference to the ground, fly in furtherance of a business, or fly outside the United States.

AN ULTRALIGHT AIRCRAFT (in the U.S.) is any powered aircraft that has only one seat, a fuel capacity of no more than 5 gallons, an empty weight of less than 254 pounds, a top speed of 64 mph in level flight, and a maximum stall speed of 27 mph. It may

be flown only during daylight hours and over unpopulated areas. Unpowered ultralight aircraft (such as hang gliders, paragliders and hot-air balloons) are limited to an empty weight of less than 155 pounds.

An ultralight pilot is not required to have a pilot certificate (license) but should still seek the guidance and direction of a competent instructor before attempting to fly an ultralight aircraft. Even though ultralight pilots are not required to be licensed, they are responsible for abiding by certain aviation regulations.

Although many **ANTIQUE AIRCRAFT** are housed in museums, many others are maintained and flown by antique buffs the world over. These aviators contend with drafty cockpits, uncomfortable accommodations, poor performance, and other conveniences because of the enjoyment they get from being intimately associated with aviation history. Many antique aircraft, however, are unstable, demanding, and difficult to fly. Flying these aircraft safely is a challenge and requires skill and experience.

This antique Bellanca Pacemaker began service with Hawaii's Inter-Island Airways in 1929.

Another antique is this Travel Air biplane.

Antique aircraft are generally considered to be aircraft designed and manufactured before the end of World War II. Included also are replicas and some later models that are the oldest of their class or one-of-a-kind aircraft. Antique aircraft typically belong in one of five chronological categories:

Pioneer Age	1903–1914
World War I	1914–1918
Golden Age	1919–1934
Classic Age	1934–1942
World War II	1942–1945

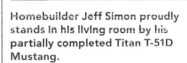
Rutan Long-EZs.

HOMEBUILT or AMATEUR-BUILT AIRCRAFT

satisfy the desires of those who prefer to design and build their own airplane instead of buying a production airplane. Others might choose to build their own airplane using a kit or instructions that can be purchased from a designer.

Homebuilders know their airplanes better than most other pilots do. They have spent innumerable hours cutting, welding, stitching, riveting, sanding, painting, forming, modeling, and bonding and assembling every one of the thousands of pieces and components that comprise the finished aircraft. Anyone not fond of such labor should not entertain the notion of building their own airplane. While the final out-of-pocket cost might be less than the cost of a comparable production airplane, the homebuilder must be dedicated to a form of self-imposed

Homebuilder Jeff Simon proudly stands in his living room by his partially completed Titan T-51D Mustang.

exile if the wings of his creation are to take flight.

Before a homebuilt airplane can be flown, it must be approved by a government inspector from the Federal Aviation Administration. This helps to protect the public from potentially unsafe aircraft. After the first test flight, the aircraft must be successfully and safely flown for a specified number of hours before the pilot may use the aircraft to carry passengers.

CHAPTER 4
AIRCRAFT ENGINES

PISTON ENGINES • OPERATING AN AIRPLANE ENGINE • ENGINE COOLING
FUEL MANAGEMENT • JET PROPULSION • JET ENGINES

PISTON (or RECIPROCATING) EN-GINES, similar to those used in automobiles, power most light airplanes. Their basic mechanism consists of a cylinder, piston, connecting rod, and crankshaft. The top end of the connecting rod is attached to the piston, which moves up and down inside the cylinder. The bottom of the rod is attached to the crankshaft, which converts the up-and-down motion of the piston to a rotary motion, which turns the crankshaft that is attached to the propeller.

At the closed (top) end of the cylinder are two spark plugs to ignite the fuel and two openings controlled by valves. One opening (the intake valve) admits a mixture of fuel and air, and the other, the exhaust valve, allows the burned gases (exhaust) to escape.

Aircraft engines are more reliable than automotive engines in several respects. They are cooled by air and not dependent on water pumps and radiators. In addition, an aircraft engine has two independent ignition systems (two spark plugs per cylinder) while an auto engine has only one. Also, the spark plugs are not dependent on an electrical system; each ignition system includes a device called a magneto that independently generates the electricity that powers the spark plugs. An aircraft engine operates without either a battery or a generator; an automobile engine cannot.

The typical engine *(above)* **used in small, general aviation airplanes is air-cooled and has four or six horizontally opposed cylinders.**

This installed engine *(right)* **also is air-cooled and has four horizontally opposed cylinders.**

A FOUR-STROKE (or FOUR-CYCLE) ENGINE operates in the following manner: **(A)** The piston moves down, the intake valve opens, and the mixture of fuel and air enters the cylinder. **(B)** Both valves close and the piston rises, compressing the fuel-air mixture. **(C)** Sparks from the spark plugs ignite the mixture. Expansion of the burning gas forces the piston downward and produces power to turn the crankshaft. **(D)** The exhaust valve opens, and the hot exhaust gases are forced out of the cylinder by the rising piston. The entire cycle is then ready to begin again.

A one-cylinder engine delivers power only once in every four strokes of the piston. The rotational momentum of the crankshaft carries the piston through the other three strokes. To increase engine power and operating smoothness, other cylinders are added and their power strokes timed to occur at successive intervals during the rotation of the crankshaft.

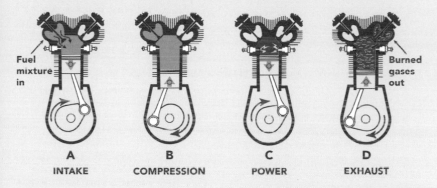

Fuel mixture in

Burned gases out

A	B	C	D
INTAKE	COMPRESSION	POWER	EXHAUST

THE CARBURETOR is where air and fuel are mixed proportionately before entering the engine cylinders. A fuel-air mixture of about 12 parts air (by weight) to 1 part fuel (12:1) is generally best. Too much fuel and insufficient air is a rich mixture that results in inefficient burning, wasted fuel, and decreased power output. Too much air and not enough fuel is a lean mixture that can cause engine overheating.

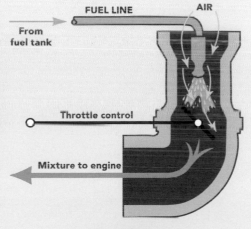

FUEL LINE

AIR

From fuel tank

Throttle control

Mixture to engine

CARBURETOR

Power controls in a single-engine airplane *(left)*. The throttle is black, the propeller-pitch control is blue, and the mixture control is red.

OPERATING AN AIRPLANE ENGINE requires more skill and knowledge than operating an automobile engine. There are many more factors to consider. These include knowing how to operate the related systems and how to keep the engine running smoothly during wide variations in altitude and temperature.

Before starting the engine, the aircraft should be in a position where the propeller will not stir up gravel or sand and cause damage, injury, or annoyance to anyone or anything behind the aircraft.

Different engines require different starting procedures, but all have two important requirements in common: (1) no one should be allowed to stand near the propeller, and (2) the oil-pressure gauge must be checked within a few seconds after start. If no pressure is indicated, the engine must be shut down immediately. Without sufficient oil pressure, an operating engine can be seriously damaged in a short time.

Prior to takeoff, all engine systems are checked for proper operation. This includes ensuring that the engine will operate satisfactorily on either of its two independent ignition systems and that the engine has warmed to normal operating temperatures.

AS THE AIRCRAFT CLIMBS, the density of the air decreases. As a result, the amount (weight) of the air entering the carburetor also decreases. The amount of fuel entering the carburetor, however, remains the same (for any given throttle setting). Consequently, the ratio of fuel to air increases—the mixture becomes too rich. The mixture control is used to reduce the amount of fuel to the carburetor, *leaning* the mixture to maintain the proper fuel-to-air mixture. The pilot must not forget to enrich the mixture during the subsequent descent into denser air. These same principles apply also when operating a fuel-injected engine.

THE PROPELLERS of most small, light planes have a fixed pitch. That is, the angle that the blades make with their plane of rotation cannot be changed. Aircraft with more powerful engines are equipped with variable-pitch propellers. Using a control in the cockpit, the pilot can change the propeller pitch to suit varying conditions for the same reasons that drivers shift gears.

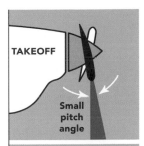

TAKEOFF

Small pitch angle

THE VARIABLE-PITCH PROPELLER operates (in principle) much like an automobile transmission. The prop *pitch* (sometimes called *bite*) is set to a small angle during takeoff to provide maximum acceleration at a high rpm (like first gear). For climb, the propeller is set to a medium pitch angle (second gear). A large pitch angle (low rpm) is used during cruise flight (third gear).

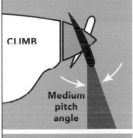

CLIMB

Medium pitch angle

COOLING AIRCRAFT ENGINES is usually done by air, the result of an airplane's forward speed. An engine can become overheated if operated at full throttle at a relatively low airspeed (as during a steep, prolonged climb on a hot day). This condition can be detected by an abnormally high indication of the oil temperature gauge. Many aircraft are additionally equipped with a cylinder-head temperature gauge that provides an earlier warning. To solve the problem, the aircraft nose is lowered somewhat to increase airspeed (which increases engine cooling), or the amount of power being used is reduced, or both.

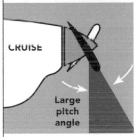

CRUISE

Large pitch angle

Some aircraft are equipped with cowl flaps that help to cool the engine at low airspeeds. These are small doors that are opened to increase airflow through the cowling (engine cover), which carries away some of the heat generated by the engine. The cowl flaps usually are not needed during cruise (high-speed) flight and are closed to reduce drag.

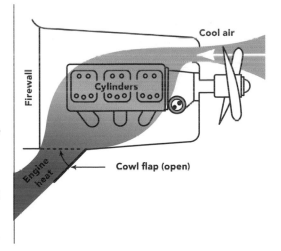

Cool air

Firewall

Cylinders

Engine heat

Cowl flap (open)

FUEL MANAGEMENT is an important consideration during every flight. Planning begins on the ground. The pilot first determines that sufficient fuel is on board for the flight to be made safely. For example, a 3-hour flight in an airplane that consumes 8 gallons of fuel per hour will require 24 gallons of fuel. An extra 30 minutes of fuel (4 gallons) is required for reserve fuel just in case the flight takes longer than estimated. Many pilots (including the author of this book) prefer never to take off without at least one hour's worth of reserve fuel.

Unlike a car, an airplane typically has more than one fuel tank, which are usually built into the wings. On a high-wing airplane, the fuel is above the engine and flows by gravity to it. The fuel in a low-wing airplane, however, cannot flow uphill and must be forced up by a fuel pump. Two pumps, one engine-driven and one electrically powered, are generally installed in low-wing aircraft to provide a backup in case one fails.

Prior to flight, each fuel tank is inspected and the fuel levels are verified visually. A pilot rarely trusts the indications of the fuel gauges. A pilot must also verify that the fuel tanks contain the proper type of fuel. Use of jet fuel in a piston engine, for example, can cause engine failure. Aviation fuel (avgas) can be distinguished from jet fuel (kerosene) by color and feel.

The Pipistrel Velis Electro, the first certified, electrically powered airplane, being charged between flights. It obviously does not use conventional fuel.

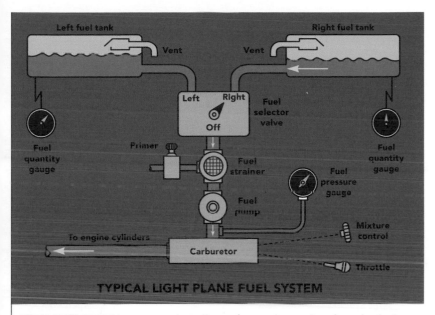

TYPICAL LIGHT PLANE FUEL SYSTEM

EACH FUEL TANK has a vent that allows air to enter and replace the fuel that is consumed while en route. The pilot inspects these vents before flight to ensure that they are not clogged. If a clogged vent goes undetected, air cannot enter the fuel tank and, as the fuel level lowers during flight, a partial vacuum is created in the tank. This suction could prevent fuel from flowing freely to the engine and cause fuel starvation and power failure.

IMPURITIES in the fuel tanks that could cause an engine power loss should be detected and eliminated before flight. Water and dirt are heavier than fuel and, if present, settle to the bottom of fuel tanks. Prior to flight, the pilot opens a drain at the bottom of each fuel tank to rid the fuel system of such impurities.

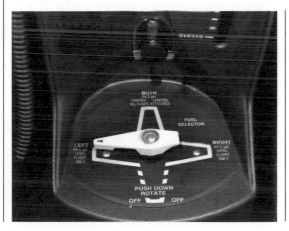

A FUEL SELECTOR is used to choose the tank that the pilot wants to use at any given time. Takeoffs and landings are made with the fullest tank supplying the engine. While en route, alternate use of the right and left wing tanks prevents the aircraft from becoming unbalanced (one wing heavier than the other).

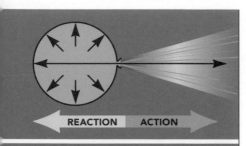

JET PROPULSION is obtained by an application of Newton's Third Law of Motion: *For every action, there is an equal and opposite reaction.*

If the air inside a balloon is allowed to escape, the balloon moves in the direction opposite to that of the escaping air. The air escaping through the nozzle is the action; the balloon's motion is the reaction.

The balloon will continue to move as long as the air pressure inside is greater than the pressure outside. When all of the air escapes, the balloon will fall and come to rest.

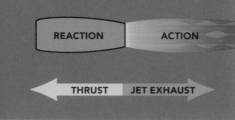

A *jet or gas turbine engine* takes in air continuously and, with the help of fuel, makes its own high pressure with which it produces power. The high-velocity exhaust provides forward thrust.

Escaping air from a balloon is an example of jet action.

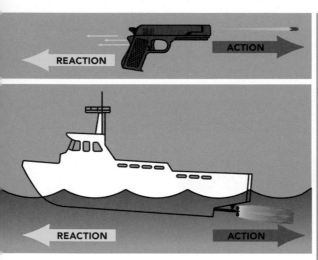

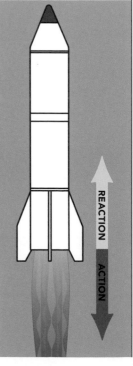

ACTION = REACTION

- The action of a jet engine is the exhaust raging out of the tailpipe, and the reaction is forward thrust.
- A shooter experiences kickback (reaction) when a bullet is fired (action).
- A ship moves forward in reaction to the water forced rearward by the propeller (action).
- A rocket rises in reaction to its exhaust (action).

THE HORSEPOWER of a jet engine cannot be expressed as a fixed number; It increases in proportion to aircraft speed. At 375 mph, 1 pound of thrust equals 1 horsepower. At 750 mph, 1 pound of thrust equals 2 horsepower. Each engine of an Airbus A380F produces up to 76,000 pounds of thrust. Each engine of a Citation CJ3 *(right)* produces 2,820 pounds of thrust.

A turboprop aircraft uses jet-engine power to turn a propeller.

THE POWER of a jet engine is expressed in pounds of thrust, and the amount of thrust (the reaction) is dependent on the mass of the exhaust and how much it is accelerated by the engine.

For example, if a 4-ounce bullet is fired from a gun with an acceleration of 960 feet per second per second, the force (action) applied to the bullet is equal to 7.5 pounds. The gun reacts (kickback) as if a 7.5-pound force had been applied to it. If the weight or acceleration of the bullet is doubled, the amount of the force (and the kickback) is also doubled (15 pounds).

A JET ENGINE is the most common type of reaction engine. It generates power by compressing air from the atmosphere to a higher pressure (as in the toy balloon discussed on page 66). This is done by the compressor section of the engine.

However, greater energy is needed than can be obtained from compressed air alone, so the compressed air is expanded by heat from burning fuel. This happens in the combustion section of the engine where a fire rages continuously once the fuel has been ignited. This fire is lighted with a spark plug (an igniter), which is not used once the engine has been started.

STAGES OF OPERATION

THE OPERATING PRINCIPLES of a jet engine can be described by the following sequence: **(A)** The air ahead of the engine is sucked in and compressed by a large fan, or compressor. **(B)** To further increase the pressure of the inlet air, additional compressors are added. **(C)** As the air is compressed, it occupies less space. This is why the compressors and the surrounding engine casing get smaller as the pressure increases. **(D)** The compressed, high-pressure air leaving the compressor section contains enough oxygen to support combustion with a very hot flame, but compressing the air also causes it to leave the compressor section at very high speed. Since this could blow out the flame, the compressed air is first slowed down by passing it through a diffuser. As the air enters the wide throat of the diffuser, it slows down, just as water from a garden hose slows when it flows through a funnel (page 15). **(E)** Some of the

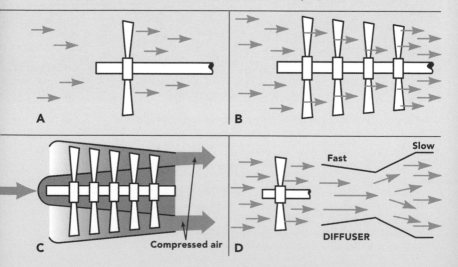

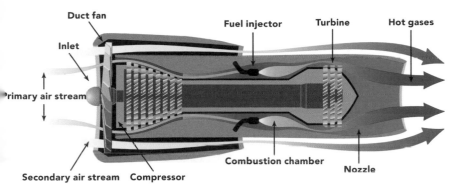

Cutaway view of a gas turbine (pure jet) engine.

compressed air is mixed with fuel to produce a fire in the combustion chamber(s). The rest is directed through the chamber to be expanded and accelerated by the heat of the fire. The hot gases then flow through a nozzle. This increases the velocity again. This raging flow of hot gases passes through a turbine wheel that spins a shaft attached to the compressor fans, thus providing power for the compressor section of the engine.

After passing through and spinning the turbine(s), the gases flow through a narrowing exhaust nozzle, which further increases their speed. The action of these high-speed exhaust gases exiting the tailpipe produces a reaction called jet thrust, which provides the aircraft with forward motion.

IN A TURBOPROP ENGINE (F), more turbine wheels are added to the engine to capture most of the energy contained within the exhaust gases. This energy is converted into shaft power that turns the propeller.

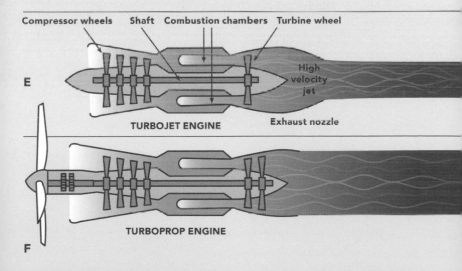

CHAPTER 5
FLIGHT INSTRUMENTS

AIRSPEED INDICATOR • ALTIMETER • ATTITUDE INDICATOR • TURN COORDINATOR
SLIP INDICATOR • ELECTRONIC FLIGHT INSTRUMENTS • COCKPIT

THE AIRSPEED INDICATOR registers the speed of an aircraft through the air. In flight, air flows into the open end of a pitot (pronounced pee-toh) tube that projects forward into the airstream. It was invented by the French engineer Henri Pitot, who originally created the device to measure the speed of a river current.

As the speed of the air increases, the pressure of the air ramming into the pitot tube increases, the way pressure increases against the palm of your hand when it is stuck out the window of an accelerating automobile. This high-pressure air passes through a long tube and forces a diaphragm inside the instrument to expand. The expanding diaphragm causes the hand on the face of the instrument to move, indicating the airspeed in knots (nautical miles per hour) or statute miles per hour (on old airplanes). In some countries, the airspeed indicator of older light airplanes is calibrated in kilometers per hour.

If an airplane dives at too high an airspeed, the tremendous air pressure created by the relative wind can cause structural damage. This is why an airplane has a maximum-allowable airspeed indicated by a red line on the face of the instrument (*right*).

Pitot tube.

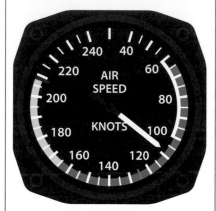

THE SPEED RANGE covered by the yellow arc is the caution range and is to be avoided during flight in turbulent air or during abrupt maneuvering.

The green arc shows the range of normal speeds. The low end of the green arc is the normal stalling speed when the flaps are up (retracted).

The white arc indicates the range of speed during which the wing flaps may be lowered. At higher speeds, air pressure could damage the flaps. The low end of the white arc indicates the normal stalling speed with the flaps extended.

AT HIGH ALTITUDES, the air is thinner (less dense) than at sea level. Consequently, air entering the pitot tube has less ram pressure, and the airspeed indicator is in error. The airspeed indicated on the face of the instrument is less than the actual or true airspeed. For example, at 10,000 feet, an airplane might have a true or actual airspeed of 300 knots but an indicated airspeed of only 258 knots. A small handheld calculator can be used to determine true airspeed based on indicated airspeed, altitude, and temperature.

Early airspeed indicators like this one are quite simple. The relative wind blows against a spring-loaded plate to which the indicator is attached.

MACH NUMBER is the airspeed of a jet-powered airplane with respect to the speed of sound. The speed of sound (determined by Ernst Mach) is 660 knots (760 mph) at sea level. An airspeed equal to the speed of sound is Mach 1.0. Flying at half the speed of sound is Mach 0.5. Speeds less than Mach 1.0 are subsonic; speeds greater than Mach 1.0 are supersonic. Hypersonic refers to a speed of Mach 5.0 or greater.

THE ALTIMETER indicates altitude above sea level, not above the ground. To determine altitude above the ground, a pilot checks the elevation of the terrain over which the aircraft is flying on an aeronautical chart. If the altimeter indicates 9,500 feet, and the terrain is 5,000 feet above sea level, the aircraft's altitude above the ground is 4,500 feet.

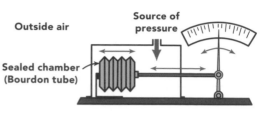

Outside air

Source of pressure

Sealed chamber (Bourdon tube)

ANEROID BAROMETER

THE ALTIMETER IS READ like a clock. The longest, thinnest pointer indicates tens of thousands of feet, and the shortest pointer indicates thousands of feet. The medium-length pointer indicates hundreds of feet. The instrument shown above indicates 2,955 feet above sea level.

The altimeter is essentially an aneroid barometer. It contains a sealed chamber that expands with an increase in altitude (because of a decrease in atmospheric pressure) and contracts during descent (because of increased pressure). This expansion and contraction of the chamber causes the altimeter hands to move. An altimeter indicates correctly only during standard atmospheric conditions. Because these rarely exist, compensations are made.

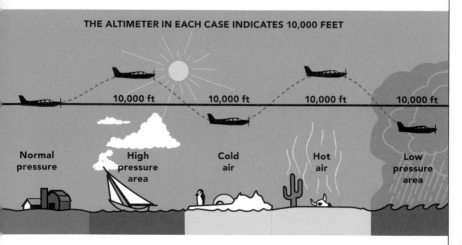

THE ALTIMETER IN EACH CASE INDICATES 10,000 FEET

10,000 ft   10,000 ft   10,000 ft   10,000 ft

Normal pressure

High pressure area

Cold air

Hot air

Low pressure area

When a pilot flies unknowingly into a low-pressure area or abnormally cold air, the altimeter indicates higher than the actual altitude—a dangerous error, as it means the aircraft is lower than the pilot thinks it is. When flying into a high-pressure area or abnormally warm air, the altimeter indicates less than the actual altitude.

THE VERTICAL SPEED INDICATOR (VSI) is closely related to the altimeter. It indicates the rate of climb and the rate of descent of an aircraft (the rate of change of altitude or vertical speed). The instrument shown here indicates that the aircraft is maintaining a constant altitude. When the needle moves clockwise, it indicates the rate of climb (such as 500 feet per minute); when it moves counterclockwise, it indicates the rate of descent.

ALTIMETER ERRORS can provide false indications. For example, assume that an airplane is at rest on a sea-level airport where the atmospheric pressure is 30.00 inches of mercury. The altimeter indicates zero. A storm soon approaches the airport, and atmospheric pressure decreases to 29.50 inches. The altimeter senses this drop in pressure and reacts as if it had been elevated to a higher altitude where that low of a pressure would normally be found. Because a half-inch decrease in pressure corresponds to a 500-foot gain in altitude, the altimeter would indicate 500 feet even though the aircraft had never left the ground.

Conversely, an increase in pressure has the opposite effect.

COMPENSATING DEVICES are built into altimeters. The pilot uses such a device to adjust the altimeter to the current sea-level pressure (usually obtained by radio) for a given location. A knob on the altimeter is twisted until the correct *altimeter setting* appears in the small window. The altimeter then indicates correctly.

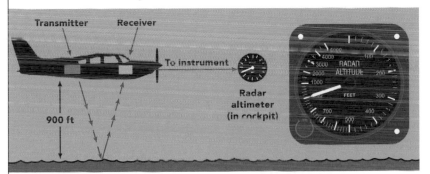

The **RADAR ALTIMETER** measures altitude above the ground (absolute altitude). It sends a radar signal earthward and measures how long it takes for the signal to bounce back to the aircraft. The absolute altitude is proportional to the time required for the signal to make a round trip and is shown on the face of the instrument.

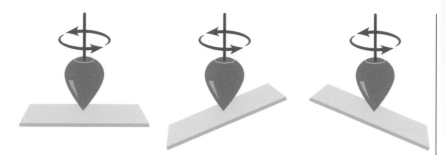

THE ATTITUDE INDICATOR operates on the principle of a gyroscope, which rotates rapidly about its own axis and tends to remain fixed in space (like the toy top in the illustration above). No matter which way its platform tilts, the top remains fixed in space. Its attitude does not change.

The attitude indicator depicts the aircraft's attitude in relation to a line representing the real (outside) horizon, which is why this instrument used to be called an artificial horizon. It shows how much an aircraft is banked (right or left) and how high or low the nose is pitched. This information is particularly important to a pilot when flying in cloudiness, a time when the real horizon cannot be seen. Controlling aircraft attitude by reference to the attitude indicator (as well as other instruments) is called *instrument flying*. Controlling aircraft attitude by reference to the real horizon by looking outside the window is called *visual flying*, or contact flying.

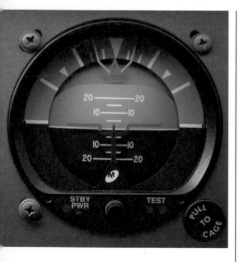

AN ATTITUDE INDICATOR contains a rapidly spinning gyroscope. No matter which way the aircraft banks or pitches, the horizon shown on the face of the instrument remains aligned with the actual horizon outside the aircraft. The small symbolic airplane on the face of the instrument remains aligned with the actual aircraft. Thus, the *artificial horizon* and the symbolic airplane combine to provide a visual of aircraft attitude. This makes it easier for pilots to control the attitude of their aircraft without being able to see the outside world. Such instrument flying used to be called blind flying.

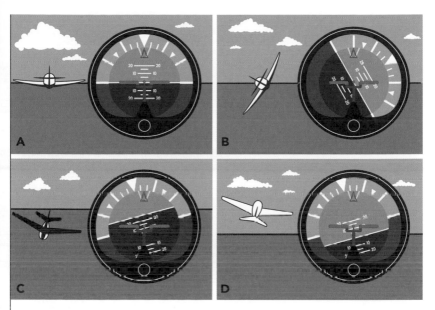

INTERPRETING an attitude indicator is not difficult. The diagrams above show how the instrument appears when an airplane is in four different attitudes: (A) The airplane is in level flight. The wings of the airplane on the instrument are parallel to the horizon, and the nose is not pitched up or down. (B) The airplane is in a 60-degree left bank, and its nose is not pitched up or down. (C) The airplane is banked 15 degrees right and is descending (the nose is below the horizon). (D) The airplane is in a 15-degree right bank and is nose high. The airplane might be climbing, or it might be mushing in slow flight. The altimeter or the vertical-speed indicator must be consulted to determine the flight condition.

THE HEADING INDICATOR is a related instrument discussed on page 123.

Air from outside the instrument is sucked through an air jet.

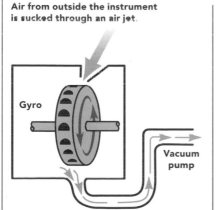

THE GYROSCOPE contained inside an attitude indicator is spun at high speed by a jet of air. Air is continuously sucked out of the instrument by an engine-powered vacuum pump that draws a stream of air into the instrument through a nozzle. This continuous blast of high-speed air spins the gyro the way water turns a waterwheel, but much faster. Some attitude indicators are electrically driven or electronically operated.

THE TURN COORDINATOR consists of two independent displays built into one: a turn indicator and an inclinometer (slip indicator).

The turn indicator contains a small gyroscope that is aligned within the instrument so as to display both roll and yaw. During straight-and-level flight, the symbolic airplane on the instrument's face displays a wings-level attitude. As the airplane is rolled into a turn, the symbolic airplane banks in the same direction. The more the symbolic airplane moves, the greater is the rate at which the airplane is rolling into the turn. Once the turn is stabilized, however, the symbolic airplane displays only the rate at which the airplane is turning.

The standard turn rate used in flying light airplanes is 3° per second. At this rate, a full circle (360°) takes 120 seconds (2 minutes). One minute is required to turn around (180°) and 30 seconds is required to make a 90° turn. (The standard rate of turn for jet airplanes is 2° per second.)

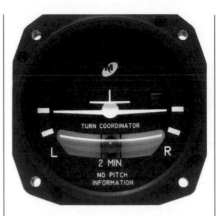

In the drawing below, **(A)** shows that the airplane is neither banking nor turning. **(B)** indicates that the airplane is in a standard turn to the left (the left wingtip of the symbolic airplane is on the hash mark representing a standard turn). **(C)** shows that the airplane is in a steep and rapid turn to the right.

Although the turn indicator has an appearance similar to that of an attitude indicator, it does not show when the airplane pitches up or down.

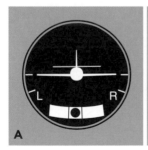

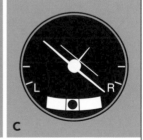

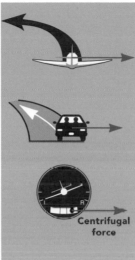
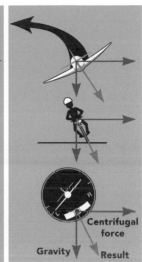

THE SLIP INDICATOR (inclinometer) shows the relationship between the airplane's bank angle and its rate of turn. The instrument consists of a curved glass tube that contains a black steel ball and is filled with kerosene to dampen the ball's movement. The ball moves as the result of natural forces that also are felt by the pilot.

The forces that act upon the slip indicator (slip-skid ball) are shown above. The automobile on the left is driving straight ahead on a road that is banked left. Gravity pulls on the driver and he leans left. The same thing happens when an airplane is banked but does not turn. The ball in the instrument falls left indicating that the left wing is low. The pilot corrects this *slip* by turning the wheel to the right and lifting the low (left) wing.

The center car is making a tight left turn on a level road. The leaning felt by the driver is the result of centrifugal force pulling him to the right. When an airplane is forced to enter a left turn with the rudder and is not banked, the same thing happens. Centrifugal force pulls the pilot and the ball in the instrument to the right. The turn indicator and the slip-skid ball show a skidding left turn. The pilot corrects this *skid* by banking into the turn or by pressing the opposite rudder pedal to stop the skidding turn.

The bicycle shown on the right is in a banked left turn. Gravity pulls on the cyclist, but this is counteracted by the centrifugal force created by the turn. As a result, the cyclist remains comfortably balanced in the seat. The same is true of a pilot (and the passengers) during a normal turn. The slip-skid ball also is balanced and remains centered.

ELECTRONIC FLIGHT INSTRUMENTS are new-generation instruments that are rapidly replacing the conventional and individual instruments found in older aircraft and shown on previous pages in this chapter. These older instruments are now colloquially referred to as *steam gauges*. The newer electronic flight instruments are computer-based, digital instruments that are presented on a single flat-screen called a *primary flight display* (PFD) that has the appearance of a computer monitor. In addition to combining the attitude indicator, heading indicator, altimeter, airspeed indicator, turn coordinator, and vertical-speed indicator in a single display, the PFD also contains additional flight information as well as an interface for operating aircraft radios used for communications and navigation.

The primary flight display is typically accompanied by a *multi-function display* (MFD) that—you guessed it—performs multiple functions. Most importantly, it contains a moving map for navigation (similar to that found in many automobiles). The MFD also can show engine instruments and displays of other important systems. These include:

- A traffic collision avoidance system (TCAS) that shows the relative location and altitude of nearby aircraft.
- A terrain awareness and warning system (TAWS) that alerts a pilot to potentially hazardous terrain.
- A display of various aeronautical charts.
- A display of pertinent weather information.
- A radar display (page 165) that shows the proximity of rain showers and thunderstorms.

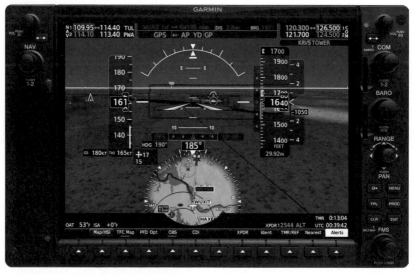

Garmin primary flight display (PFD).

Garmin multi-function display (MFD).

An aircraft with a primary flight display and a multi function display is colloquially referred to as having a *glass cockpit* because the instrument panel is dominated by glass displays. Such an aircraft also is called a technically advanced aircraft (TAA) because the digital instrumentation and autopilot are more advanced than aircraft with steam (analog) gauges.

An in-flight failure of a primary flight display or multi-function display could, of course, create a hazardous situation. Because of this

possibility, each flat-screen display has a reversionary mode. Should the PFD fail, for example, the information previously displayed there would automatically appear on the MFD but in a somewhat compressed fashion, and vice-versa.

Such aircraft also have some conventional instruments to serve as an emergency backup as well as supplemental electrical systems to prevent an electrical failure from turning off all of the electronic flight instruments.

THE COCKPIT is the pilot's front office and is loosely analogous to the driver's station in an automobile. Larger cockpits often are called flight decks. The pilot-in-command (captain) typically sits on the left while a flight instructor, copilot, or passenger sits on the right. Each of the pilots is usually equipped with a control wheel (or control stick or sidestick) to operate the ailerons and elevator. The pilot uses rudder pedals on the floor to operate the rudder. Other controls are provided to operate the wing flaps and the trim tabs.

Small supplemental panels are used to cluster together switches with similar purposes. For example, one such panel might contain light switches, while another might contain radio and electronic switches. The throttle and other engine controls most often are clustered in a quadrant on the lower, center portion of the instrument panel in a way that provides both pilots with easy access to these controls.

Instrument panel with conventional, analog gauges.

In this glass cockpit *(above)*, the primary flight displays (PFDs) on the left and right provide primary flight information for each pilot. The multi-function display (MFD) in the center provides a moving-map display and other navigational information for both pilots.

CHAPTER 6
FLIGHT MANEUVERS

STRAIGHT-AND-LEVEL FLIGHT • TURNS • CLIMBS • GLIDING
TAXIING • TAKEOFF • LANDING • INSTRUMENT FLYING • AEROBATICS

STRAIGHT-AND-LEVEL FLIGHT (or cruise flight) may be defined as a series of recoveries from slight turns, dives, and climbs. To be more accurate, it is flying in a given direction at a constant altitude with the wings level.

In smooth air and when properly trimmed, an airplane's stability theoretically enables it to maintain straight-and-level flight by itself. In reality, though, a pilot must make slight corrections with the flight controls to maintain the desired altitude and direction. For example, a ripple in the air might cause the left wing to lower slightly; the pilot, holding the control wheel lightly, applies right aileron pressure to restore level flight. Similarly, if the nose rises slightly, the pilot applies slight forward pressure on the control wheel to return the airplane to its normal pitch attitude.

Straight-and-level flight can be maintained by referring to the flight instruments, but most pilots prefer to use the natural, outside horizon as a reference. For example, the pilot can tell whether the wings are level simply by looking at them relative to the horizon.

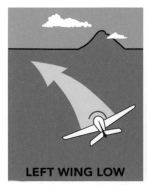

LEFT WING LOW

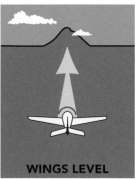

WINGS LEVEL

RIGHT WING LOW

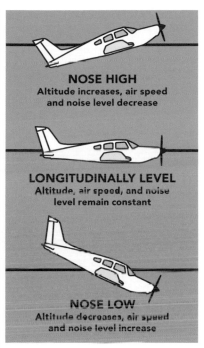

NOSE HIGH
Altitude increases, air speed
and noise level decrease

LONGITUDINALLY LEVEL
Altitude, air speed, and noise
level remain constant

NOSE LOW
Altitude decreases, air speed
and noise level increase

An automobile driver increases and decreases speed with the accelerator (gas pedal) to adapt to varying driving conditions. In straight-and-level flight, a pilot is seldom required to vary airspeed. The engine throttle is set in one position. Unlike the automobile's accelerator, the airplane throttle does not spring back to the idle position.

Although a compass can be used to maintain a constant heading, most pilots use this instrument only to establish the airplane in the desired direction. Then they maintain flight in that direction by aiming at a distant point (such as a mountain). If one wing becomes low, a gradual turn develops. This is easily detected as the nose of the airplane moves to the right or left of the aiming point. The pilot knows which wing is low by the direction of the turn and applies corrective control movements.

PITCHING, nose up or nose down, is controlled by the elevator. The pilot learns by experience where the nose should be relative to the horizon and keeps it there during straight-and-level flight.

If the nose is held too high, the aircraft enters a shallow climb, noticeable on the altimeter. As the nose begins this upward flight, the airspeed decreases just as the speed of an automobile decreases when it is driven uphill (unless the driver gives it more gas). This is shown on the airspeed indicator, but an experienced pilot can sense a drop in airspeed simply by the decreasing sound level of the relative wind passing by the aircraft. A nose-high attitude is corrected by a forward nudge on the control wheel. Conversely, if the nose goes down slightly, the aircraft enters a shallow dive; altitude decreases and airspeed increases (more air noise).

TURNS are of three types, depending on bank angle: shallow (20 degrees or less), medium (20 to 45 degrees), and steep (45 degrees or more).

To begin a left turn, for example, the control wheel is turned left, which moves the ailerons and rolls the airplane into a left bank. This use of ailerons alone, however, causes an undesirable yaw to the right. To counteract or prevent this yaw, it is necessary to press gently on the left rudder pedal while the ailerons are being used. If insufficient rudder is applied, the airplane *slips*; if too much rudder is used, the airplane *skids (see below)*.

It is important to understand that the rudder does not turn the airplane as it does on a boat. Banking the airplane (tilting the force of wing lift) creates the turning force (page 32). The rudder on an airplane is a form of trimming device that assists the ailerons in performing their job more effectively. When the desired bank angle is reached, the ailerons and rudder are neutralized.

NORMAL TURN
Correct amount of rudder used to enter turn.

SKIDDING TURN
Results from using excessive rudder to enter a turn.

SLIPPING TURN
Results from using insufficient or opposite rudder to enter a turn.

A properly trimmed airplane in a medium-bank turn in smooth air tends to continue turning without assistance once the desired bank angle is established.

Some of the wing's lift is used to turn the airplane (page 32). Unless additional lift is somehow obtained, an airplane loses altitude in a turn. Back pressure applied to the control wheel to increase the wing's angle of attack creates the additional lift necessary to maintain altitude in a turn. To enter a turn properly, therefore, it is necessary to coordinate the use of all three primary flight controls: ailerons, rudder, and elevator.

As the desired direction of flight is approached during a turn, the pilot recovers from the turn by again coordinating the movement of ailerons and rudder, but this time they are applied opposite to the direction of turn. For example, recovery from a left turn requires turning the control wheel to the right and applying pressure to the right rudder pedal. As the bank angle decreases, back pressure on the control wheel is also decreased.

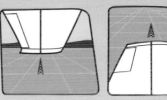

High wing

Low wing

The *around pylon* is a training maneuver. The pilot selects a point on the ground and attempts to fly a constant-radius circle around it while maintaining a constant altitude and airspeed. This shows the pilot's view from the window of both a high-wing and low-wing aircraft while performing the around pylon maneuver.

PLACEMENT OF THE AILERONS AND RUDDER:
(A) Entering, (B) maintaining, and (C) recovering from a left turn

A   B   C

This STOL (short takeoff and landing) airplane is designed specifically to take off from and land on short runways. It also is capable of climbing and descending at steep angles. The unique wing of a STOL airplane is capable of developing lift sufficient to remain safely airborne at relatively slow speeds.

CLIMBS are of two basic types, normal and maximum performance. In the *normal climb*, the airplane is flown at an airspeed that results in it climbing at its best (greatest) rate of climb, gaining the most amount of altitude in a given period of time. In the *maximum-performance climb*, the airplane is flown at an airspeed that results in it climbing at its best (steepest) angle of climb, gaining the most altitude in a given distance over the ground.

The normal climb is entered from straight-and-level flight by applying gentle back pressure to the control wheel. As the nose rises, airspeed begins to decrease. The throttle is advanced simultaneously. When the normal, slower climb speed is reached, the pilot maintains that speed by varying back pressure on the control wheel as necessary. During a climb, the engine/propeller combination in most airplanes, especially single-engine airplanes, creates a force that causes the airplane to yaw to the left. The pilot counteracts this yaw to keep the airplane on a constant heading by applying sufficient pressure on the right rudder pedal.

As the airplane approaches the altitude desired by the pilot, the nose is lowered slightly to decrease the rate of climb and to allow airspeed to increase. When the target altitude is reached, the nose is lowered further to stop the climb and to allow the aircraft to accelerate to its cruising speed. When cruising speed is reached, the throttle is retarded to the power setting needed for cruise flight.

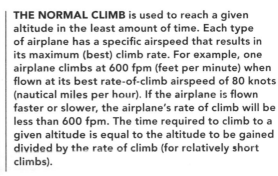

THE NORMAL CLIMB is used to reach a given altitude in the least amount of time. Each type of airplane has a specific airspeed that results in its maximum (best) climb rate. For example, one airplane climbs at 600 fpm (feet per minute) when flown at its best rate-of-climb airspeed of 80 knots (nautical miles per hour). If the airplane is flown faster or slower, the airplane's rate of climb will be less than 600 fpm. The time required to climb to a given altitude is equal to the altitude to be gained divided by the rate of climb (for relatively short climbs).

Towplane and glider immediately after liftoff. Look carefully to see the towline connecting the two aircraft.

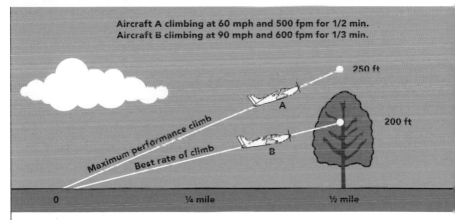

Aircraft A climbing at 60 mph and 500 fpm for 1/2 min.
Aircraft B climbing at 90 mph and 600 fpm for 1/3 min.

250 ft

200 ft

Maximum performance climb

Best rate of climb

0   ¼ mile   ½ mile

THE MAXIMUM-PERFORMANCE CLIMB is used to climb over tall obstacles such as trees or power lines at the departure end of a runway. The pilot is not concerned with the time required to gain altitude but rather with climbing at the steepest angle possible to gain the most altitude in a given horizontal distance. This is done by climbing at a slower airspeed. Even though the aircraft is climbing at a relatively low rate of climb (compared to a normal climb), the airplane's relatively slow speed over the ground gives it more time to clear the obstacle.

A GLIDE is a controlled, power-off descent. Contrary to popular belief, an airplane without power does not dive out of control and into a spin (as some motion pictures might lead you to believe). Instead, the airplane simply glides as if it were a glider. With the throttle retarded (engine idling), the typical light airplane descends at approximately 500 feet per minute. If the pilot of such an airplane begins gliding from an altitude of 10,000 feet, the airplane can glide for 20 minutes (10,000 ÷ 500 = 20) before reaching the ground (assuming that it is at sea level). If forced to glide as the result of an engine failure, a pilot usually has ample time to select a suitable landing area to make a safe, forced landing.

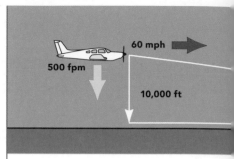

There are many factors to consider if a forced landing is to be successful. For example, when landing on a plowed field, land parallel to the furrows, not across them. When flying over bodies of water, remain high enough to glide to shore in case of an engine failure.

A glide can be an important phase of an approach to a normal landing, too. When an aircraft gets within gliding distance of the runway, the pilot can glide to a point immediately above the runway where the landing sequence is begun.

Every airplane has an optimum gliding speed that allows it to glide a maximum forward distance. Assume that the airplane shown in the illustration above has an optimum gliding speed of 60 mph. During each minute of gliding flight, the aircraft glides forward one mile (60 mph = 1 mile per minute) and loses 500 feet of altitude. The ratio of horizontal distance flown to altitude lost (5,280 feet ÷ 500 feet) is the airplane's *glide ratio*, which in this case is 10.6 to 1. This means that for every 10.6 feet the aircraft moves forward, it loses one foot of altitude. The larger the glide ratio of an airplane, the greater is its *gliding efficiency*. Some high-performance gliders have glide ratios in excess of 50 to 1. Such a glider (or sailplane) can glide 50 miles from an altitude of only 1 mile (5,280 feet).

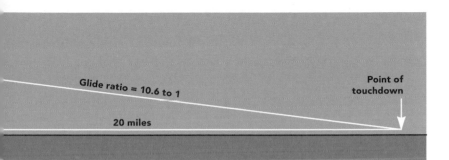

Glide ratio = 10.6 to 1

20 miles

Point of
touchdown

GLIDING EFFICIENCY decreases if an airplane is flown slower or faster than its optimum glide speed. At too low an airspeed, the wing is at too large an angle of attack, and additional drag impedes forward motion. At too high an airspeed (diving), the airplane descends so rapidly that it reaches the ground before it has had time to fly very far.

Gliding at the optimum speed is especially important if an engine fails (in a single-engine airplane). This allows the pilot to glide the greatest horizontal distance over the ground and increases the choice of landing sites. An aircraft at 10,000 feet with a glide ratio of 10.6 to 1 can glide 20 miles in any direction, and its pilot has a choice of landing sites anywhere within a 1,256-square-mile area.

When NASA's Space Shuttle left orbit to return to Earth, it did so without power. In other words, it glided all the way from a low Earth orbit to its designated landing site. During flight at hypersonic speeds (more than 5 times the speed of sound), the orbiter has a glide ratio of only 1.05 to 1. (It descends at about a 45-degree angle.) When subsonic (less than the speed of sound), it has an improved glide ratio of 5.1 to 1—which is still a far cry from that of a jetliner, which typically has a 20 to 1 glide ratio.

TAXIING a light airplane is not done with a steering wheel. Directional control is maintained by moving the rudder pedals, which are connected to the steerable nosewheel or, in the case of a *taildragger*, to the tailwheel. Pushing the right rudder pedal with your right foot turns the aircraft to the right; pushing the left pedal with the left foot turns it to the left. Airliners have a special steering control called a tiller.

Forward speed is controlled with engine power. The brakes on most airplanes are controlled also with the rudder pedals. These brakes are applied by depressing only the tops of the pedals. To avoid inadvertently applying these brakes while steering, foot pressure is applied only against the bottom portions of the pedals.

The brakes can generally be applied to one wheel at a time (right or left) to assist in making a sharp turn in the desired direction. Application of both brakes simultaneously stops the aircraft.

Airplanes on the ground are not as stable as automobiles. An airplane has only three wheels, and its weight (center of gravity) is higher off the ground. Fast, sharp turns on the ground can tip a small plane and damage a wingtip (an accident called a ground loop).

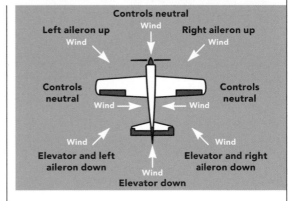

In a taildragger airplane *(above)*, the rudder pedals are connected to the tailwheel for steering on the ground. This type of aircraft is not as stable as one with tricycle landing gear. Maintaining directional control during the takeoff roll in a taildragger requires almost constant corrective movement of the rudder pedals.

Controls neutral

Left aileron up
Wind

Wind

Right aileron up
Wind

Controls neutral
Wind

Wind

Controls neutral

Wind

Wind

Elevator and left aileron down

Wind

Elevator and right aileron down

Elevator down

A pilot must be cautious when taxiing in strong winds. To prevent the wind from raising a wing, the nose, or the tail, the pilot applies the flight controls as shown, depending on wind direction.

WHEN A PILOT TAXIS into a tight or unfamiliar parking area, an attendant often provides guidance using standardized hand signals *(below)*. This attendant, or marshaller, stands in a location that provides a line of sight to both wingtips and all surrounding obstacles. At night, the marshaller uses illuminated wands to direct the pilot.

START ENGINE   RIGHT TURN   LEFT TURN   MOVE AHEAD

ALL CLEAR (OK)   SLOW DOWN   IDLE ENGINE   CUT ENGINE

STOP   INSERT WHEEL CHOCKS   PULL WHEEL CHOCKS   EMERGENCY STOP

THE TAKEOFF is the beginning of flight and requires enough lift from the wings to overcome aircraft weight. This is best accomplished by taking off directly into the wind (upwind). In this way, air flows over the wings (the airplane has airspeed) even before the takeoff roll has begun, and less runway distance is needed to become airborne. A takeoff generally is not made with a tailwind (downwind) because of the additional runway distance this requires.

When cleared for takeoff, the pilot taxis the airplane onto the runway, advancing the throttle slowly and smoothly in one continuous motion until the engine is developing maximum power. The rudder pedals, which are linked to a steerable nosewheel or tailwheel, are used to maintain directional control and remain on the centerline of the runway.

The airplane is ready for takeoff when it has accelerated to the appropriate airspeed. Some pilots think that they can sense when the airplane is ready for takeoff by the way it feels or responds to small control movements. However, this is not an appropriate way to manage a takeoff. If the pilot forces the airplane into the air at too slow a speed, it might settle back to the runway.

As the airplane accelerates, the pilot holds the control wheel in an approximately neutral position if it is an airplane with tricycle landing gear. If flying a tailwheel airplane, the pilot applies some forward pressure on the control wheel to raise the tail and position the airplane in an approximately level attitude. This reduces drag and enhances acceleration.

When flying speed is reached, the pilot applies gentle back pressure to the control wheel. This raises the nose, poises the airplane for flight, and provides for a smooth and safe liftoff. The pilot then allows the airplane to accelerate to the airspeed needed for a normal climb, raises the nose farther to maintain that speed, and climbs straight ahead until reaching a safe altitude.

Pilot's view of runway while on short final approach to landing.

THE LANDING is not necessarily the most difficult maneuver to perform, yet it is the one that most pilots try to perfect more than any other (perhaps because pilots are most frequently judged by their landings). The pilot of a light plane normally begins the landing approach with a normal glide to the runway at anywhere from 1 to 3 miles away at an altitude of 800 to 1,000 feet above the ground. (When flying larger aircraft, some power is used to prevent too rapid a descent.)

During the approach, if the pilot determines that the airplane is too low and will undershoot the runway, engine power is used either to reduce the rate of descent or to temporarily maintain altitude. If the pilot sees that the airplane is too high and will overshoot the runway, he or she can reduce power further and lower the wing flaps. Flaps allow the airplane to descend more steeply without developing excess airspeed. If the airplane is still too high, the pilot executes a go-around by climbing and circling the airport for another try.

The pilot normally lands into the wind to effect a slower groundspeed (page 118) at touchdown. When the airplane descends to within 5 to 10 feet above the runway, the pilot gradually changes the aircraft's

| NORMAL GLIDE | BEGINNING OF THE FLAREOUT | FLOATING ABOVE THE RUNWAY |

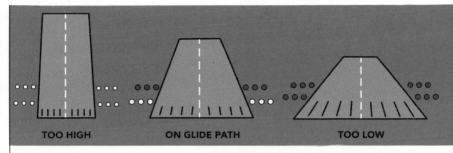

TOO HIGH   ON GLIDE PATH   TOO LOW

Many runways are equipped with a *visual approach slope indicator* (VASI) system. It consists of 12 lights that provide pilots with a visual flight path to the approach end of the runway. If an airplane is coming in too high (above the normal glide path), all VASI lights are white. If the aircraft is too low (below the normal glide path), all lights are red. When an aircraft is on the normal glide path, the far set of lights is red, and the near set of lights is white. Smaller airports have similar but simpler approach lighting systems.

attitude from that of a normal glide to a somewhat nose-high attitude. This stops the descent rate in a manner that allows the airplane to float immediately above and parallel to the runway. This change of aircraft attitude and flight path is called the landing flare.

The pilot begins the flare with gentle back pressure on the control wheel, which increases pitch attitude and dissipates airspeed. The back pressure is continued smoothly, just enough to prevent the airplane from contacting the runway prior to it reaching the landing attitude. When the landing or touchdown attitude is achieved, the airplane is only

inches above the runway and close to stalling. At this point, the airplane touches down.

If the landing flare is performed too aggressively, the airplane will balloon, resulting in an undesirable gain in height. If the flare is performed too slowly, the airplane plops onto the ground while descending and might bounce back into the air. Learning to land requires finesse and lots of practice.

After the airplane is on the ground and rolling along the runway, the pilot maintains directional control with the rudder pedals and smoothly applies the brakes.

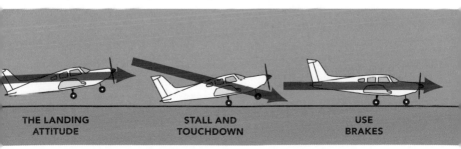

THE LANDING   STALL AND   USE
ATTITUDE   TOUCHDOWN   BRAKES

Instrument flying skills are needed to fly safely when the natural horizon and the ground cannot be seen, such as when flying in cloudiness or thick haze.

A pilot learning "blind" (instrument) flying in a flight simulator.

INSTRUMENT FLYING is an important skill. On the ground, our senses—particularly vision—help us to maintain balance and determine direction and motion. When flying, however, unless pilots can see outside the aircraft, their senses will mislead and confuse them about the attitude and behavior of the aircraft. This is exactly what happens when clouds or poor visibility obscure outside references. A pilot's senses cannot be relied upon at such times to determine which way the airplane might be turning or if it is climbing or descending.

Pilots can ignore their senses and use the airplane's flight instruments as a way to perceive what the airplane is doing with respect to the outside world.

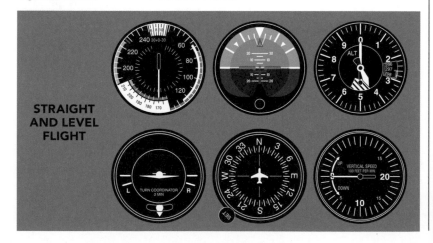

STRAIGHT AND LEVEL FLIGHT

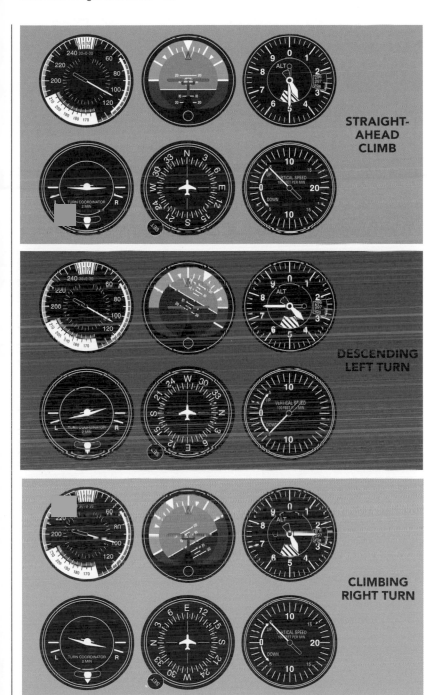

STRAIGHT-
AHEAD
CLIMB

DESCENDING
LEFT TURN

CLIMBING
RIGHT TURN

Many aerobatic maneuvers are mild, such as the lazy eight. However, it is not easy to perform them well. Smooth coordination of constantly changing flight-control movements is required. Maneuvers such as the outside loop can tax aircraft and pilots to their structural and physiological limits. In extreme cases, pilots can encounter *red-out* (in which their eyes literally see red). This apparently is due to the lower eyelid acting as a red curtain over the eye, and it occurs when centrifugal forces cause excess blood to flow from the lower to the upper extremities.

AEROBATICS consist of maneuvers requiring either abrupt attitude changes or attitudes exceeding more than 60 degrees of bank or 30 degrees of pitch. Such maneuvers can place heavy strain on a pilot or an aircraft, but these are not required to obtain a pilot certificate (license). Aerobatic maneuvers are performed only by those interested in developing these specialized skills.

A blackout can occur during a rapid pull-up from a steep, high-speed dive. The pilot is forced hard against the seat by a combination of gravity and centrifugal force, causing blood to leave the pilot's head. This can temporarily result in a partial (gray-out) or complete (blackout) loss of vision.

OTHER MANEUVERS—such as spins, loops, and rolls—are safe, fun, and pose no hardship to pilots and aircraft qualified to perform them. Sustained inverted flight is possible only in aircraft modified to provide fuel and oil to the engine when the aircraft is upside down. If an unmodified airplane is flown inverted for more than several seconds, fuel and oil starvation can cause engine failure.

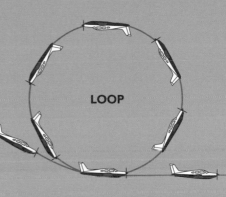

LOOP

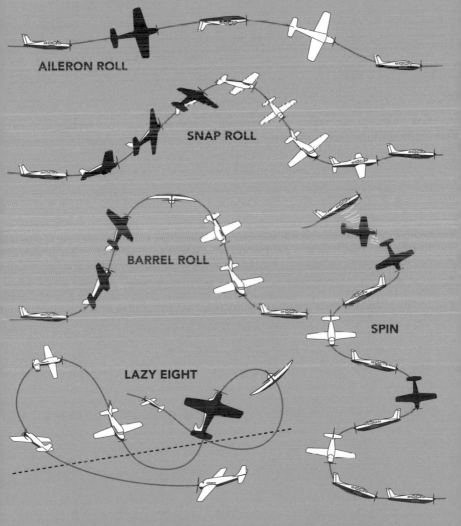

AILERON ROLL

SNAP ROLL

BARREL ROLL

SPIN

LAZY EIGHT

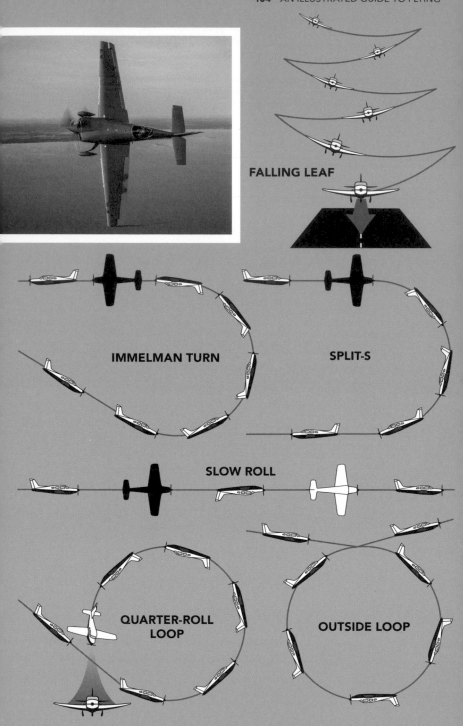

FALLING LEAF

IMMELMAN TURN

SPLIT-S

SLOW ROLL

QUARTER-ROLL LOOP

OUTSIDE LOOP

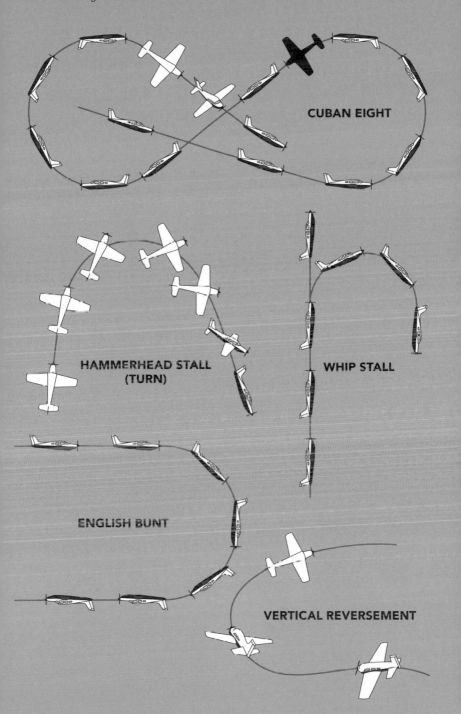

CUBAN EIGHT

HAMMERHEAD STALL (TURN)

WHIP STALL

ENGLISH BUNT

VERTICAL REVERSEMENT

CHAPTER 7
BASIC NAVIGATION

THE EARTH'S COORDINATES • AERONAUTICAL CHARTS
SPECIAL USE AIRSPACE • ESTABLISHING DIRECTION • PLOTTING COURSES
PILOTAGE • AIRSPEED AND GROUNDSPEED • AIRCRAFT HEADING
MAGNETIC COMPASS • MAGNETIC VARIATION AND DEVIATION • COMPASS HEADING

Any point on Earth can be described by a system of coordinates, but since there are no visible reference lines, we use imaginary ones. On a curved surface such as the Earth, which is a sphere, we use circles.

THE EQUATOR is an imaginary circle—halfway between the North and South Poles—that divides the Earth into the Northern and Southern Hemispheres. Circles parallel to the Equator are called parallels of latitude.

THE EARTH'S COORDINATES

provide a means of describing the exact position of any point on Earth. For example, the location of a local gas station might be given as being precisely 5 blocks north of Maple Street and 3 blocks east of Elm Street in Happyville, California. The numbers 5 and 3 give position with respect to two reference lines (the streets); the reference lines are called coordinates.

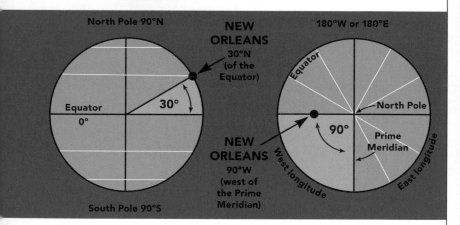

The longitude of New Orleans is 90°W, which when combined with its latitude of 30°N, gives a precise description of its location on Earth.

EACH PARALLEL of LATITUDE is designated by its angular distance north or south of the Equator. A point on the Equator has a latitude of 0°. As the distance of a point increases north or south of the Equator, its latitude increases. The latitude of the North Pole is 90°N, and the latitude of the South Pole is 90°S. New Orleans, Louisiana, is about a third of the distance between the Equator and the North Pole, or 30° north of the Equator; its latitude is 30°N.

MERIDIANS OF LONGITUDE are drawn from the North Pole to the South Pole and are perpendicular (at right angles) to the Equator. The meridian passing through Greenwich, England, is called the Prime Meridian. It is the Earth's other reference line.

Each meridian is designated by its angular distance east or west of the Prime Meridian. Any point on the Prime Meridian has a longitude of 0°. As the distance of a point on the Earth increases east or west of the Prime Meridian, its longitude increases. The longitude on the opposite side of the Earth from the Prime Meridian is 180°E or 180°W. This is the International Date Line.

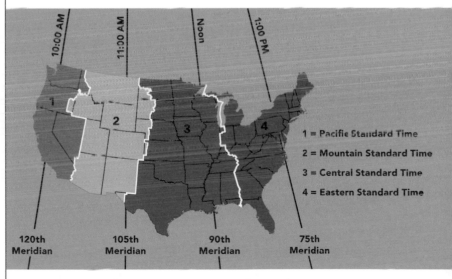

1 = Pacific Standard Time
2 = Mountain Standard Time
3 = Central Standard Time
4 = Eastern Standard Time

The Earth is divided into 24 time zones, one for each 15° change in longitude. The contiguous United States spans four of these zones.

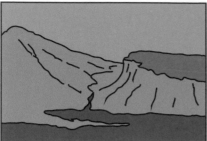 

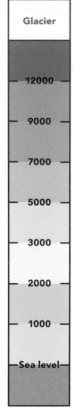

Different color tints on aeronautical charts represent different areas of elevation relative to sea level.

AERONAUTICAL CHARTS are maps intended for use in aerial navigation. It would take a book of at least 100 pages to offer the same information that is displayed on one chart using standardized symbols. The shapes, sizes, and colors of these symbols are designed to look much like the Earth's features that they represent.

THE SECTIONAL AERONAUTICAL CHART is used primarily for flight in visual conditions and is the most popular aeronautical chart used in the United States. These charts are called sectional charts because each covers a specific section of the country. Thirty-seven of them cover the 48 states, sixteen are needed for Alaska, and one covers the Hawaiian Islands. Sectional charts have a scale of 1:500,000, which means that one inch on the chart represents a half-million inches on the ground. In other words, one inch on the chart equals approximately 8 statute miles (7 nautical miles).

A chart has only two dimensions yet must accurately represent the Earth's three dimensions. Land elevations are portrayed with contour lines (illustrated above) that are emphasized by colored tints. For example, as shown in the key on the left, the terrain between 1,000 and 2,000 feet above sea level is represented by a green tint. The terrain between 2,000 and 3,000 feet above sea level is represented by a pale yellow tint, and so forth.

When contour lines are close together, this means that the terrain represented rises sharply. When they are far apart, the elevation change is gradual.

CHART SYMBOLS

(Relief and Hydrography Features)

Spot elevation

Contours

Depression

Hachures

Bluffs, cliffs, escarpments

Lava flows

Sand or gravel areas

Sand ridges

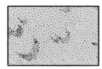
Sand dunes

Levees and eskers

Shorelines

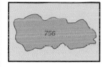
Lakes

Lakes (dry/intermittent)

Lakes (numerous small)

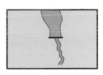
Dams

Rivers and streams (perennial)

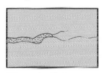
Rivers and streams (seasonal)

Swamps, marshes, bogs

Land subject to inundation

Canals (regular, to scale, abandoned)

Springs, wells, waterholes

Salt pans (evaporator)

Rapids and falls

Glaciers

Tidal flats (exposed at low tide)

Reefs (coral or rocky)

Mountain pass

SECTIONAL AERONAUTICAL CHART LEGEND (excerpts)

Airports with control towers shown in blue; all others in magenta.

AIRPORT SYMBOLS

○ ○ Other than hard-surfaced runways

⚓ Seaplane Base

◐ ⊗ Hard-surfaced runways 1500 ft to 8069 ft in length

◢ ✛ Hard-surfaced runways greater than 8069 ft, or same multiple runways less than 8069 ft.

◔ ✛ Open dot within hard-surfaced runway configuration indicates approximate VOR, VOR-DME, or VORTAC location.

Ⓡ Private Airport

◎ ◎ Military Airport

Ⓗ Heliport Selected

Ⓤ Unverified

⊗ Abandoned-paved, having landmark value. 3000 ft or greater

Ⓕ Ultralight Flight Park Selected

◈ ○ ⚓

Services—fuel available and field attended during normal working hours depicted by use of ticks around basic airport symbol. (Normal working hours: Mon–Fri, 10:00 a.m.–4:00 p.m.)

☆ Rotating airport beacon in operation Sunset to Sunrise

OBSTRUCTIONS

Λ 1000 ft. and higher AGL

Λ below 1000 ft AGL

Λ or Λ Group Obstruction

Λ or Λ Obstruction with high-intensity lights May operate part-time

2049 ← Elevation of the top above mean sea level

(1149) ← Height above ground

UC ← Under construction or reported; position and elevation unverified.

AIRSPACE INFORMATION

▬▬ Class B Airspace

▬▬ Class C Airspace (mode C See FAR 91.215/AIM.)

– – – – Class D Airspace

[40] Ceiling of Class D Airspace in hundreds of feet.

– – – Class E (sfc) Airspace

▬▬ Class E Airspace with floor 700 ft above surface.

▬▬ Class E Airspace with floor 1200 ft or greater above surface that abuts Class G Airspace.

|||||||||| Prohibited, Restricted, and Warning Areas; Canadian Advisory, Danger, and Restricted Areas.

|||||||||| Alert Area and MOA (Military Operations Area)

///// Special Airport Traffic Area (See FAR Part 93 for details.)

•°•°•° ADIZ (Air Defense Identification Zone)

▬▬ Mode C (See FAR 91.215/AIM)

▬ ▬ National Security Area

▬▬ Terminal Radar Service Area (TRSA)

←IR211 MTR (Military Training Route)

TOPOGRAPHIC INFORMATION

95 / 40 Roads & Road Markers

+—+—+—+ Railroad

⟊ ⟊ Power Transmission Lines

■– – –■ Aerial Cable

■ Landmark Feature (stadium, factory)

◆CG Coast Guard Station

• Tank—water, oil, or gas

○ Oil Well   • Water Well

⚒ Mine or Quarry

‿ Mountain Pass 11823 (Elevation of Pass)

FOR EXAMPLE ONLY. DO NOT USE FOR NAVIGATION. FOR CURRENT CHARTS, SEE FAA.GOV.

SPECIAL-USE AIRSPACE is plainly marked on aeronautical charts used for visual navigation and should be taken into consideration when planning a flight.

A pilot may not fly into a **prohibited area** under any circumstances, usually for reasons of national security. Prohibited areas protect such places as the White House, the Pentagon, etc.

Restricted areas are blocks of airspace normally reserved for use by the military. They frequently contain hazards not possible to see with the naked eye, such as fired artillery shells, machine-gun bullets, missiles, and rockets. Pilots may fly through restricted areas when it can be determined that such airspace is not in use. They also may fly over the *ceiling* or under the *floor* of some restricted areas (as indicated on an aeronautical chart). Some restricted areas are only in use by the military during specified published hours. At other times, a pilot may fly through such a restricted area.

Warning areas contain hazards similar to those found in restricted areas but are located over water that is near the coast of the United States.

Military operations areas (MOAs) are blocks of airspace used by the military for pilot training, practicing bomb runs, dogfighting, aerobatics, etc. Pilots may fly through MOAs but should exercise extreme caution while doing so.

Alert areas also require transiting pilots to exercise extreme care because of the activities that can occur there. These include parachute jumping, glider operations, hang-glider activity, and ultralight aircraft activity.

Temporary flight restrictions (TFRs) are areas where flight is restricted to protect persons or property on the ground. Because they usually are temporary, TFRs normally are not published on aeronautical charts.

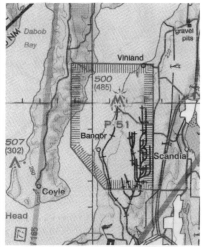

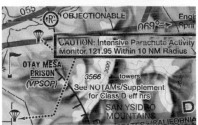

Aeronautical charts showing prohibited area around the U.S. Naval Submarine Base at Bangor, Washington *(top)* and parachute activity warning *(bottom)*.

ESTABLISHING DIRECTION is no problem when your goal is in sight. To get to a neighbor's house across the street, you simply turn toward that house and begin walking. However, establishing direction visually cannot be done when flying from Los Angeles to Hawaii, for example, because Hawaii cannot be seen from Los Angeles. Pilots have the problem of determining in which direction to point their airplanes.

In navigation, north is called *true north* and is the direction of the North Pole from any point on Earth. South is the direction of the South Pole. When facing north, east is to your right, and west is to your left. The intermediate directions also have names such as northeast, southeast, southwest, and northwest. But there are only a small number of named directions, and the names can be cumbersome to use in navigation.

The system used in aviation navigation is simpler. Direction is expressed as an angle measured clockwise from true north. Imagine a circle drawn about any location, and its circumference is divided into 360 equal units (degrees). These divisions are then numbered clockwise from true north and indicate true directions from the center of the circle. Such a circle is called a *compass rose*. The direction of north is 000 or 360 degrees (000° or 360°), east is 090 degrees (090°), south is 180 degrees (180°), and west is 270 degrees (270°).

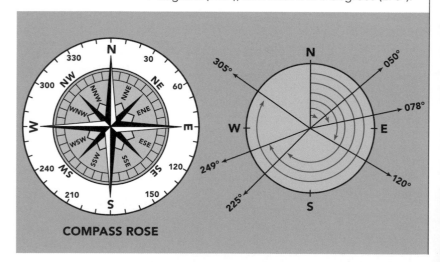

COMPASS ROSE

PLOTTING COURSES is done prior to departing on a flight. The pilot connects the departure and destination points with a straight line on an aeronautical chart. This line represents the proposed flight path and is called the *true course* because its direction is measured with reference to true north. (The desired flight path might be a series of shorter true courses because a dogleg sometimes is safer or more practical than a direct route.)

A plotter *(right)* is a protractor combined with mileage scales. It is used to measure the direction of the true course (or courses), which is the clockwise angle formed at the intersection of a meridian and the course line. The true course from A to B *(below)* is 070°. The return flight (the reciprocal course from B to A) has a true course of 250°.

The distance of the proposed flight is determined by measuring the length of the true course with the appropriate mileage scale on the plotter.

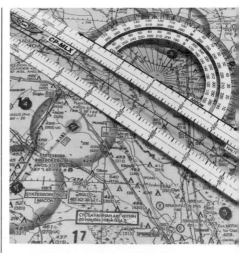

THE NAUTICAL MILE (6,080 feet) is the standard unit of distance used for aviation navigation, and it relates to the Earth's coordinate system. One degree of latitude anywhere on Earth equals 60 nautical miles (NM). A knot is a unit of speed and is 1 NM per hour. The statute mile (5,280 feet) is occasionally used, and 1 statute mile per hour is expressed as 1 mph. A nautical mile is 15 percent longer than a statute mile, and a knot is 15 percent faster than 1 mph.

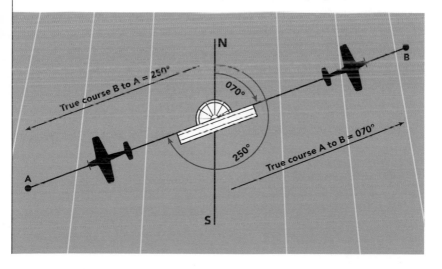

PILOTAGE is the most basic form of navigation. It is flying from one place to another by visually identifying checkpoints on the ground with those shown on an aeronautical chart. It is similar to driving a car by following directions such as "Drive along Elm Street until passing the fire station, turn right and continue along Pine Street until passing the first movie theater on the left. Take the first fork to the right...."

In the air, a pilot might fly due east until crossing a particular river, turn 30° right and fly in that direction until passing abeam an identifiable mountain, turn left 10° until passing over a kidney-shaped lake with a dam at its north end, etc.

Prior to flight, a pilot plots a course (page 115). This includes inspecting the route (as shown on the chart) with respect to potential enroute landing areas and the nature of the terrain. For example, if the intended course lies over a 12,000-foot mountain or passes through a military operations area, the pilot might elect to plot a slightly longer, dogleg course through low-elevation

Lakes and other bodies of water are indicated with a blue color on charts.

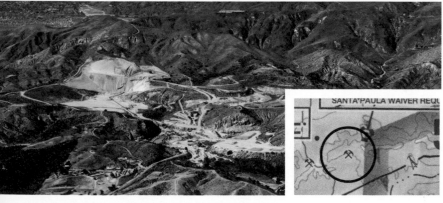

Shaft mines or quarries are depicted with a hammer and pickaxe symbol.

terrain to the south. After deciding on the best (safest) route, the pilot chooses the checkpoints to be used for navigation. Some of the best are lakes, rivers, and mountains, each with its own unique shape. Other checkpoints, such as a road passing through a small town, often are not as good. Identifying the correct road-town combination can be difficult because so many of them look alike from the air.

The key to successful pilotage is using more than one checkpoint to establish aircraft position. For example, when passing abeam a lake that appears to be the one on the chart, the pilot should then look for a second checkpoint. If the second checkpoint is also shown on the chart in proper relation to the first, the pilot has confirmed the airplane's position.

Some pilots prefer not to plot and follow courses but would rather follow a highway or a set of railroad tracks shown on the chart. Enroute checkpoints are still used to confirm position along the way.

Highways and roads are indicated with single or double, heavy black lines.

Small and nontowered airports are depicted in magenta; larger towered airports are depicted in blue.

AIRSPEED AND GROUNDSPEED are seldom equal. *Airspeed* is the speed of an aircraft through the air; *groundspeed* is its speed over the ground. They differ because of the effect of wind.

Consider the effect of wind on a balloon that has no motion of its own. At the time a balloon is launched (released to rise into the air), assume that the wind is blowing from the west at 30 mph. One hour later, the balloon will be over a point 30 miles east of its departure (launch) point. It has floated over the ground at a speed of 30 mph, which is its groundspeed (speed over the ground).

Because the balloon has no means of propulsion, its speed relative to the surrounding air is 0 mph, which is its airspeed. A balloonist never feels a breeze because the balloon is suspended in the air and moves with it. Since the balloon has no airspeed, no air moves past the balloonist. A balloon in the air is like an empty bottle floating down a river. Each travels with the current. Any free object in the air moves with the wind. This is as true of an airplane as it is a balloon. If an airplane is flying within an air mass (wind) moving at 20 mph, the airplane moves at 20 mph with it. This movement is separate from the forward movement of the airplane through the air (its airspeed). Therefore, when a 150 mph airplane flies with a 30 mph tailwind, its groundspeed is determined by combining both movements and is 180 mph. If the airplane turns around and maintains a 150 mph airspeed (its movement through the air), the 30 mph headwind causes its groundspeed to decrease to 120 mph.

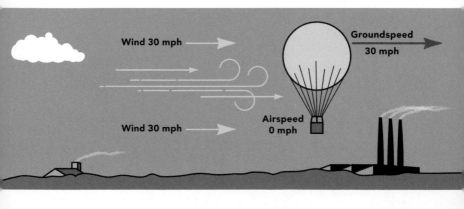

Wind 30 mph

Groundspeed 30 mph

Wind 30 mph

Airspeed 0 mph

Prior to flight, a pilot obtains a forecast of the winds aloft (the wind speed and direction forecast for various altitudes and locations) to determine what groundspeed to expect after departure. Knowing the groundspeed and the distance to be traveled, the pilot can compute an ETE (see terms below) using the formula: *Time (T) = Distance (D) ÷ Groundspeed (GS)*. Adding the ETE to the time of departure provides the ETA.

As a flight progresses, a pilot can use the following formula to calculate the airplane's actual groundspeed based on the time required to fly any given distance (between checkpoints): *GS = D ÷ T*. This is necessary because the actual wind experienced on a flight can be different than the forecasted wind conditions. Knowing the groundspeed, a pilot can estimate more accurately how long it will take to fly to distant checkpoints and to his destination. This is known as *dead-reckoning navigation* (from "deduced reckoning").

Terms Commonly Used

ETA	Estimated time of arrival
ATA	Actual time of arrival
ETE	Estimated time en route
ATE	Actual time en route
ETD	Estimated time of departure
ATD	Actual time of departure

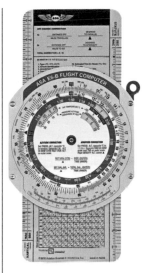

TIME-SPEED-DISTANCE computers are circular slide rules specifically designed to assist pilots in solving navigational problems. These devices eliminate the need to perform multiplication and division with pencil and paper.

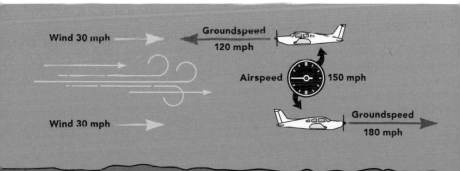

WIND DRIFT causes an aircraft to move over the ground the same way that a boat crosses a river. If the river has no current and the boat is rowed perpendicular to the river's edge, it ends up at a point on the opposite shore directly across from the starting point. If there is a current, the boat is carried (or drifts) downstream somewhat before reaching the opposite shore. The distance downstream depends upon the speed of the current and the speed of the boat.

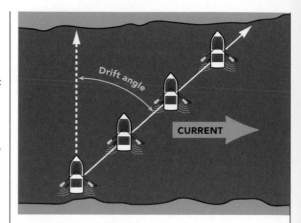

AIRCRAFT HEADING is the direction in which an airplane points. If the heading is measured with respect to true north, it is called the *true heading*. The actual flight path of an aircraft over the ground (a result of the motion of the aircraft and of the wind) is called the *track*. The angle between the heading (where the airplane is pointing) and the track (where the airplane is going) is the *drift angle*. The pilot's goal is to fly so that the track (actual flight path) coincides with the true course (intended flight path).

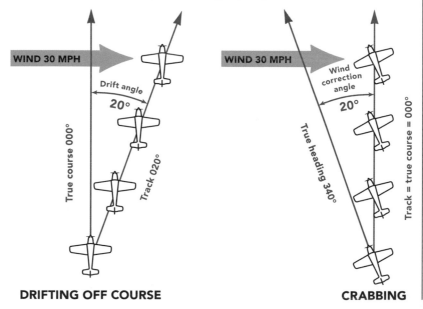

DRIFTING OFF COURSE

CRABBING

When an airplane flies in a crosswind, it drifts downwind the way a boat drifts downstream. This explains why an airplane can point (head) one direction yet travel (track) in another.

Assume that a pilot wants to fly north; the true course is 000°. The pilot turns the aircraft to a true heading of 000°. The pilot is unaware, however, that the wind at the aircraft's altitude is blowing from the west (a left crosswind) at 30 mph. As a result, the aircraft drifts to the right and flies along a track of 020°. After an hour, the aircraft will be 30 miles off course.

A pilot can counteract the effect of a crosswind. For example, knowing that a given wind can cause 20° of right drift, the pilot heads the aircraft 20° to the left; this *wind correction angle* is equal and opposite to the drift angle. Instead of flying on a heading of 000° to go north, the pilot flies on a heading of 340° (000° or 360° − 20° = 340°). This is called *crabbing into the wind.*

PLOTTING A WIND TRIANGLE solves the problem of determining the precise effect of the wind. Because the wind can blow from any of 360 directions, a direct headwind, a direct tailwind, or a direct crosswind is unusual. The wind is usually a combination of a crosswind and a headwind or tailwind. Plotting a wind triangle is an involved procedure but is much simplified using a wind-triangle computer or specialized electronic calculator *(above).*

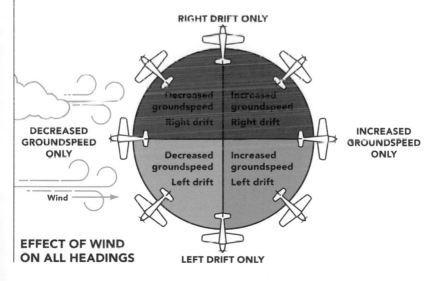

EFFECT OF WIND ON ALL HEADINGS

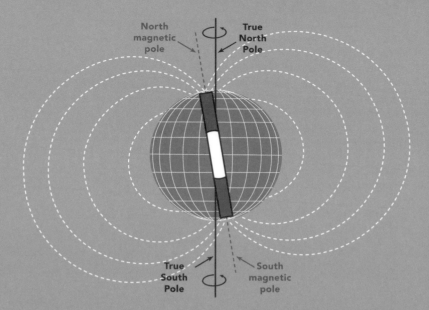

North magnetic pole

True North Pole

True South Pole

South magnetic pole

THE MAGNETIC COMPASS is an instrument used for determining direction and relies upon the Earth, which is like a giant bar magnet with north and south magnetic poles. The compass is a magnetized, slender rod that is pivoted at its middle. It rotates until one end points toward the Earth's magnetic north pole. The end that points north is called the magnet's north pole.

The magnetized rod of the aircraft compass is attached to a nonmetallic cylinder called a compass card. This card is marked every 5° of direction and numbered every 30°. A reference line, the lubber's line, is fixed on the face of the instrument case. The case is filled with liquid that steadies the card during flight. This fluid partially floats the card yet allows it to turn freely within the instrument case. As the aircraft turns, the lubber's line moves around the card, while the card itself continues to point north.

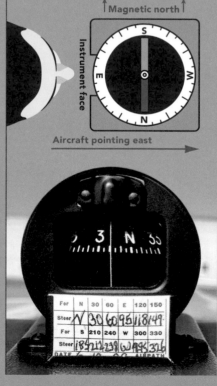

↑ Magnetic north ↑

Instrument face

Aircraft pointing east →

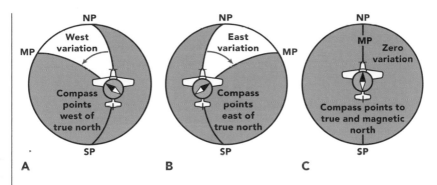

A   **B**   **C**

MAGNETIC VARIATION is an error that arises because the locations of the Earth's magnetic poles do not coincide with the locations of its geographic poles. The compass points to magnetic north, but navigation is done with respect to true north. When magnetic north and true north are in the same direction from a given point on Earth, there is no variation. Magnetic variation, therefore, varies with the location of the aircraft (*above*).

DEVIATION, another compass error, is caused by magnetic influences within the aircraft, such as electrical circuits, radios, lights, tools, the engine, and magnetized metal parts. These influences can cause the compass to *deviate* from its normal reading. Deviation varies with every airplane, with every compass, and when flying on different headings.

Aircraft **A** is at a point on Earth where magnetic north appears west of true north (westerly variation). Aircraft **B** is where magnetic north appears east of true north (easterly variation). Aircraft **C** is uniquely positioned; there is no variation.

THE HEADING INDICATOR is set to the direction indicated by the compass when the aircraft is in smooth, level flight. It then provides a steady, gyroscopically stabilized reference of direction during maneuvers and turbulence when the magnetic compass can become erratic and difficult to read.

THE NATIONAL WEATHER SERVICE provides information necessary for proper flight planning. After plotting and measuring the true course, the pilot obtains a telephone or online briefing that provides forecasted weather and winds aloft for the proposed flight. Using the wind information, the pilot determines how many degrees the airplane must be crabbed into the wind to prevent drifting off course.

THE COMPASS HEADING is the direction used (with respect to the aircraft compass) to fly a direct course from A to B. It is determined by measuring the direction of the true course with a plotter (page 115) and applying the effects of three variables: wind (page 120), magnetic variation (page 123) and compass deviation (page 123).

Assume that the measured true course is 080°, and the pilot determines that it will be necessary to crab 5° left to counter the left crosswind and stay on course. This results in a true heading of 075°.

The next consideration is to determine the amount of magnetic variation that exists in the vicinity of the proposed route of flight. The amount of variation for all localities is shown on aeronautical charts with red, dashed (isogonic) lines that connect all points of equal magnetic variation.

By referring to the aeronautical chart, the pilot locates the isogonic line nearest the intended route of flight, notes the amount of variation, and subtracts easterly (or adds westerly) variation from the true heading to arrive at the magnetic heading. If the pilot is flying over southern California with a true heading of 075°, the 13° of easterly variation results in a magnetic heading of 062°. The final step is to correct the magnetic heading for compass deviation, which is determined from the compass deviation card in the aircraft.

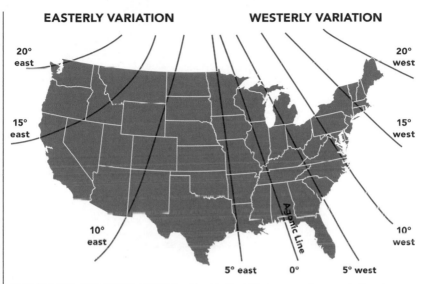

EASTERLY VARIATION   **WESTERLY VARIATION**

THE MAJOR ISOGONIC LINES for the United States are shown on the above map. A pilot compensates for 15° of easterly variation when flying over northern California and compensates for 10° of westerly variation when over Pennsylvania. The dividing line between easterly and westerly variation is the agonic line, or line of zero magnetic variation. A compass located anywhere along the agonic line points toward both the magnetic north pole and the true North Pole. There is no variation.

THE COMPASS DEVIATION CARD (*below*) indicates that to fly on a magnetic heading of 060°, a pilot must steer a compass heading of 057°. This compensates for the −3° error of this compass when heading in that direction. When heading north or south (using this particular compass), there are no deviation errors to consider. When on a magnetic heading of 270°, the pilot steers on a compass heading of 274° to compensate for the +4° of compass error.

COMPASS DEVIATION CHART

For (magnetic)	N	30	60	E	120	150
Steer (compass)	0	28	57	86	117	148

For (magnetic)	S	210	240	W	300	330
Steer (compass)	180	212	243	274	303	332

CHAPTER 8
RADIO NAVIGATION

RADIO WAVES • VOR NAVIGATION • USING VOR
DISTANCE MEASURING EQUIPMENT • MARKER BEACONS
INSTRUMENT LANDING SYSTEM • SATELLITE NAVIGATION AND GPS
INERTIAL NAVIGATION SYSTEM

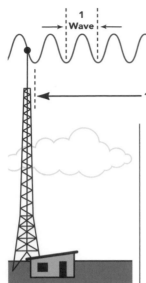

1 Wave

Wave crests

Wave troughs

12 CYCLES (WAVES) PER SECOND

The frequency of the radio signal above is 12 waves (or cycles) per second. This is expressed as 12 Hertz (Hz).

RADIO allows pilots to communicate by voice with ground stations and pilots in other aircraft. It also provides methods of navigation for when the ground cannot be seen or when flight takes place over terrain where there are no checkpoints. It also provides more accurate navigation even when ground references are visible.

Radio signals travel in waves, like those that form when a pebble is dropped in water. Radio waves, however, travel at the speed of light (186,000 miles per second). The frequency of a radio signal is determined by the number of waves transmitted each second. One thousand waves used to be called one kilocycle but is now called one kilohertz (kHz) in recognition of the German physicist Heinrich Hertz, who was first to conclusively prove the existence of electromagnetic (radio) waves. One million waves per second is called a megahertz (MHz).

Sound travels at extremely low frequencies (0.02 to 20 kHz), frequencies that can be heard with our ears. Light, on the other hand, travels at extremely high frequencies, between 360 and 780 million megahertz. Our eyes are uniquely suited to receive these frequencies and provide us with vision.

Radio Frequency Bands

VLF	Very-low frequency	10–30 kHz
LF	Low frequency	30–300 kHz
MF	Medium frequency	300–3,000 kHz
HF	High frequency	3–30 MHz
VHF	Very-high frequency	30–300 MHz
UHF	Ultra-high frequency	300–3,000 MHz
SHF	Super-high frequency	3,000–30,000 MHz

RADIO WAVES travel at frequencies that are higher than sound yet much lower than light: from 10 kHz to 30,000 MHz. This large range of radio frequencies is divided into bands (see page 128).

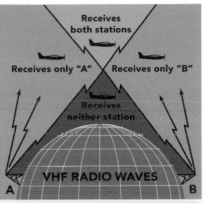

THE VHF BAND (very high frequencies) is used almost exclusively for radio communications and some radio navigation because these frequencies are rarely affected by atmospheric disturbances. Reception is usually free of static. VHF radio waves, however, can be received only when an aircraft is within *line of sight* of the transmitting station. Consequently, reception range (distance) increases with altitude *(see table below)*.

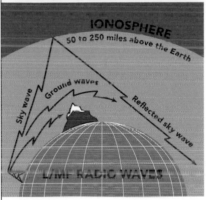

L/MF (low and medium frequencies) have been used at times for radio navigation, and this is the frequency band used by commercial broadcast stations. Reception distance does not depend on aircraft altitude. These radio waves closely follow the curvature of the Earth and can reach an aircraft (or a car radio) parked behind a distant mountain. L/MF transmissions also contain sky waves *(left)* that bounce off the ionosphere (above the stratosphere) to Earth, thus increasing reception distance, especially at night. Reception quality, however, is frequently hampered by static interference caused by atmospheric disturbances.

Aircraft Altitude	VHF Reception Distance
1,000 feet	55 miles
1,500 feet	65 miles
2,000 feet	75 miles
2,500 feet	85 miles
5,000 feet	110 miles
10,000 feet	150 miles
15,000 feet	185 miles
20,000 feet	210 miles
30,000 feet	255 miles
40,000 feet	290 miles
50,000 feet	320 miles

VOR NAVIGATION is the most common method of radio navigation utilizing ground-based stations. A VOR station is a very-high frequency (VHF) transmitter that sends beams called radials in all directions. The station is like the hub of a bicycle wheel, and the transmitted radials are like the spokes. Theoretically, a VOR station transmits an infinite number of radials, but in practice only 360 of them are usable. Each radial is identified by its direction from the station. For example, the radial transmitted due west from a VOR station is the 270° radial, and the one transmitted due south is the 180° radial.

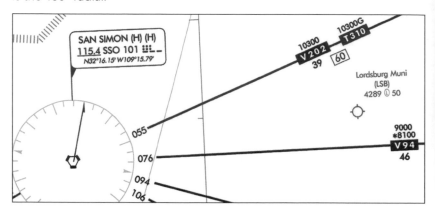

AERONAUTICAL CHARTS show the locations of VOR stations. One such station, the San Simon VOR in southeastern Arizona, is shown above. The station is located at the center of the compass rose surrounding it. If all 360 radials were depicted, the chart would be blackened with lines. Instead, only a few radials are shown, and these are segments of airways (aerial highways) that pilots can follow the way automobile drivers follow highways. For example, the 055° radial defines Victor Airway 202 (V202). Shown also is the minimum safe altitude for that airway segment (10,300 feet above sea level) plus additional coded information.

The International Morse Code

A	• —	J	• — — —	S	• • •
B	— • • •	K	— • —	T	—
C	— • — •	L	• — • •	U	• • —
D	— • •	M	— —	V	• • • —
E	•	N	— •	W	• — —
F	• • — •	O	— — —	X	— • • —
G	— — •	P	• — — •	Y	— • — —
H	• • • •	Q	— — • —	Z	— — • •
I	• •	R	• — •		

A COURSE SELECTOR (right) translates radio information into directional information. The left–right needle indicates aircraft position as it relates to the selected VOR radial. A pilot should never rely on the navigational information provided by a VOR station until aurally identifying the station being used. In the case of the San Simon VOR (shown on the preceding page) the identification is SSO (in Morse code), which is dot-dot-dot, dot-dot-dot, dash-dash-dash.

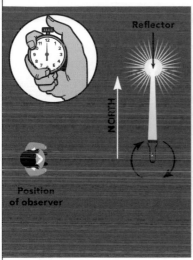

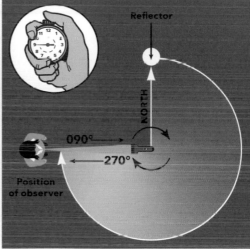

THE PRINCIPLE OF VOR navigation is explained here to correlate with the illustration above.

A revolving flashlight makes one revolution per minute. Therefore, it turns at the rate of 6° per second (360° ÷ 60 seconds = 6° per second.) A reflector is due north of the flashlight. An observer, who can see only the reflector, wants to know his direction (or bearing) from the flashlight. As the beam sweeps in a circle and briefly illuminates the reflector, the observer activates a stopwatch. At this moment, the beam is pointed north. The beam of light sweeps past the observer 45 seconds later. The observer concludes that he is west of or 270° from the flashlight (45 seconds × 6° per second = 270°). This means that the flashlight is east of or 090° from the observer.

A VOR STATION is similar in principle to this beam-reflector combination, but instead of providing directional information with a beam of light, the VOR station transmits phased radio signals. A VOR receiver in the aircraft receives these signals and passes them to the course selector (top) on the instrument panel in the aircraft's cockpit. This instrument converts the signals into directional information. The pilot twists a knob on the course sector until the left–right needle centers. The aircraft's direction to or from the station is read opposite the arrow on the compass rose surrounding the instrument.

DETERMINING AIRCRAFT POSITION using VOR navigation requires two sources of information. It is not enough to say that an aircraft is, for example, on the 180° radial of the Las Vegas VOR. The aircraft could be anywhere along that radial (south of the station). That is comparable to saying that a truck is parked on Hollywood Boulevard without giving a cross-street reference.

Aircraft position can be determined using intersecting radials in the same way that motorists use intersecting streets to describe a location. For example, the pilot in the illustration below tunes to the Los Angeles VOR and finds that the aircraft is on the 050° radial (northeast of Los Angeles). The pilot then tunes in the Ontario VOR, which indicates the aircraft is somewhere on the 310° radial (northwest) of that station. Therefore, the pilot's aircraft is at the intersection of the two radials.

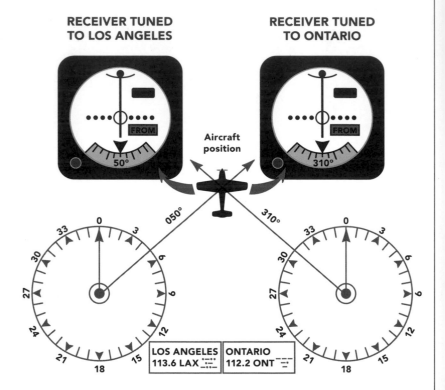

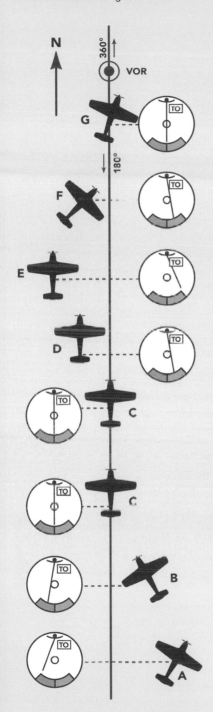

FLYING TO A VOR STATION is described and illustrated in the following steps (A through G):

A pilot at position A wants to fly to a station by following the 180° radial. But flying in that direction (south) would fly the aircraft away from the station. Instead, the pilot must fly the opposite (reciprocal) course, 360°, to get to the station.

(A) The pilot tunes in the station and rotates the course selector to 360°. The left–right needle (also called a course-deviation indicator) deflects left. This indicates that the pilot must fly left (toward the west) to intercept the desired (selected) course.

(B) As the aircraft approaches the course, the needle moves toward the center of the instrument.

(C) When the aircraft intercepts the selected course, the needle centers. The pilot turns right to a heading of 360° to remain on course. The needle remains centered as long as the aircraft remains on the radial.

(D) As the aircraft progresses, it encounters a right crosswind that causes it to drift left of course.

(E) As the aircraft drifts farther left, the needle deflects right, indicating that the pilot must turn right to return to the desired course.

(F) The right turn returns the aircraft to the selected course.

(G) Again on course, the aircraft is crabbed into the crosswind to prevent drifting off course again.

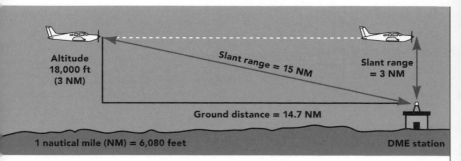

Altitude
18,000 ft
(3 NM)

Slant range = 15 NM

Slant range
= 3 NM

Ground distance = 14.7 NM

1 nautical mile (NM) = 6,080 feet

DME station

DISTANCE MEASURING EQUIPMENT (DME) automatically and electronically provides the distance (in nautical miles) between an aircraft and a DME-supported VOR station (not all VOR stations have DME). The DME equipment in an aircraft consists of a distance indicator and a UHF transmitter and receiver. The transmitter sends out interrogating signals that actuate a transponder at the selected station. This causes reply signals to be sent back to the aircraft receiver.

Because radio waves travel at a constant speed (186,000 statute miles per second), the elapsed time between the transmission and the reception of signals is proportional to the distance between the aircraft and the station. This (very small) elapsed time is measured electronically and translated into the distance of the aircraft from the station. This distance is then displayed on the DME indicator. Because the distance measured is the direct distance to the station, DME measures slant range, not ground distance. In the example illustrated above, when the DME indicates 15 nautical miles (NM), the aircraft is only 14.7 ground miles from the station. When the aircraft is 18,000 feet directly over the station, slant rage is 3 NM, yet ground distance to the station is zero.

THIS INSTRUMENT is more than a DME indicator. By measuring the rate of change of distance to or from a station, it also provides groundspeed (in knots). A small, built-in computer shows how long it will take to fly to the station based on indicated distance and groundspeed. Simple DME indicators, however, provide only distance to the station.

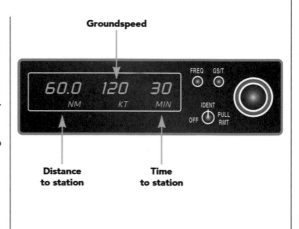

Groundspeed

60.0   120   30
NM   KT   MIN

FREQ GS/T

IDENT

OFF   PULL
        RMT

Distance
to station

Time
to station

MARKER BEACONS mark the position of an aircraft as it progresses along a specific route. The marker beacon transmitter on the ground sends a narrow vertical beam skyward; the signal is not transmitted horizontally in all directions as are most other radio transmissions. Consequently, a pilot receives a marker beacon's transmission only when the aircraft is flying through the vertical beam and is approximately above the transmitter. The pilot is made aware of passing through the marker beacon's vertical beam by an aural signal and a flashing light from a display in the aircraft.

Marker beacons used to be situated along airways. These made pilots aware of progress along their route of flight. A marker beacon might have been used, for example, to warn a pilot when the aircraft was approaching high terrain (especially valuable at night). A pilot flying in the opposite direction along that same airway would have passed over that same marker beacon, indicating that the aircraft had flown beyond the high terrain.

Nowadays, however, marker beacons are used almost exclusively to mark an aircraft's progress as it proceeds along the approach course to a runway. These are most useful when approaching an airport in cloudiness or poor visibility that prevents a pilot from seeing the runway until it is quite close.

Passing over the *outer marker* indicates that a pilot has begun the final approach to the runway. This is indicated aurally by a steady stream of low-pitched dashes (and visually with a flashing blue light). Passing over the *middle marker* informs the pilot that the aircraft is a mile or less from the runway threshold. This is indicated aurally by a medium-pitched stream of alternating dots and dashes (and visually with a flashing amber light). Finally, passing over the *inner marker* warns a pilot that the aircraft is about to cross the runway threshold, indicated aurally by a rapid and high-pitched stream of dots (and visually with a flashing white light).

THE INSTRUMENT LANDING SYSTEM (ILS) enables a pilot to make a precise approach to a runway during poor visibility when the runway cannot be seen during the approach. The landing itself is made by visual reference to the runway when the pilot gets close enough to see it. The pilot is aided in establishing visual contact with the runway by bright approach and runway lights. (If the airplane is equipped with an autopilot function called autoland, the landing can be made automatically even when the runway cannot be seen.)

The ILS incorporates two radio beams. The localizer is a beam transmitted along the extended centerline of the runway. It provides lateral (left-right) guidance to the runway. The glide slope is a beam typically transmitted at a 3° angle to the ground. It furnishes vertical guidance along the correct descent angle to the runway. Outer, middle, and sometimes inner markers (page 135) pinpoint aircraft location at two and sometimes three critical positions during an ILS approach to a runway.

Runway approach lighting system showing green threshold lights.

The **COURSE DEVIATION INDICATOR (CDI)** shows the position of an aircraft relative to the correct approach slot. The horizontal needle indicates whether the aircraft is above, below, or on the glide slope. The vertical needle indicates whether the aircraft is on course or to the left or right of course. The goal is to fly so as to keep the needles centered to the extent possible. Some indicators use a different style of needle that swings from one end (rather than shifting parallel to the center), as shown in the example on the next page.

THE VERTICAL NEEDLE *(below)* swings left and right to indicate whether the aircraft is on course **(3)**, to the right of the localizer **(4 and 5)**, or to the left of the localizer **(1 and 2)**.

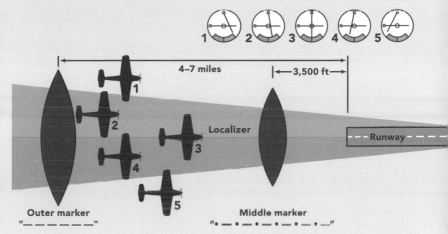

THE HORIZONTAL NEEDLE *(below)* swings up and down to indicate whether the aircraft is on the glide slope **(3)**, below the glide slope **(1 and 2)**, or above the glide slope **(4 and 5)**.

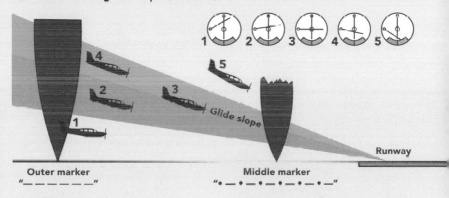

FOUR TYPICAL INDICATIONS of the ILS needles when the aircraft is neither on course (on the extended centerline of the runway) nor on the glide slope (on the proper descent path) are shown below. Indications **(1)** and **(2)** show that the aircraft is to the right of course, but in **(1)** it is too high, and in **(2)** it is too low. Indications **(3) and (4)** show that the aircraft is to the left of course, but in **(3)** it is too high, and in **(4)** it is too low.

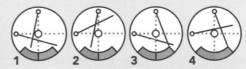

EACH SATELLITE is solar-powered and contains a transmitter and an atomic clock that keeps track of the time within a nanosecond (a billionth of a second). These ultra-high-frequency (UHF) transmitters can be received only by receivers that are on (or above) the surface of the Earth and that are within line-of-sight of the satellites. In other words, only those satellites visible (above the horizon) to an aircraft can be used for navigation.

SATELLITE NAVIGATION (satnav) is a space-based system of radio navigation. The first such system was developed by the U.S. Department of Defense and is called the *Global Positioning System* (GPS). Other satellite navigation systems have been and are being developed by other nations. For example, Russia developed and uses GLONASS, the world's second satellite navigation system.

THE GLOBAL POSITIONING SYSTEM consists of 24 satellites (plus spares) that orbit the Earth at an altitude of 12,600 statute miles and at speeds of 9,000 mph. Their orbits are arranged so that a pilot flying an aircraft equipped with a GPS receiver can receive navigational signals from at least 4 satellites at any given time, no matter the aircraft's location. Typically, however, a pilot can receive radio signals from 6–10 satellites at a time. The pilot does not have to select which satellites to use; this ongoing process is done automatically by the GPS receiver (whether in an airplane, in an automobile, on a ship, or contained in a smartphone).

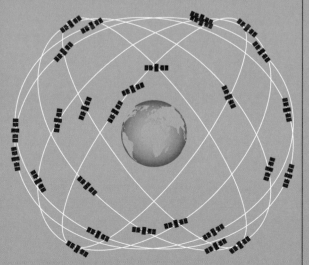

DETERMINING LOCATION WITH GPS incorporates a process called trilateration. It is based on a GPS receiver always knowing the exact location, and exact distance away, of each satellite being used at any given time. GPS receivers used in aviation are remarkably accurate and can provide geographic location to within a few feet. Explaining how GPS works in three dimensions can be difficult, but a two-dimensional example simplifies the concept and provides a sense of how GPS determines aircraft position.

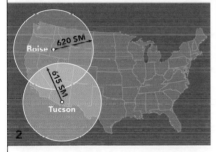

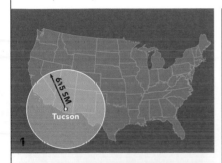

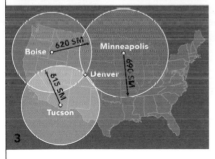

(1) Suppose a pilot has no idea of his current location. However, the pilot is informed that he is 615 miles from Tucson, Arizona. This means that the aircraft is somewhere on a circle centered on Tucson with a radius of 615 miles.

(2) The pilot is then advised that the aircraft is 620 miles from Boise, Idaho. This means it could be anywhere on a circle centered on Boise with a radius of 620 miles. Because the aircraft also is on the Tucson-centered circle, it must therefore be at one of the two points common to both circles (either near the coast of California or somewhere in Colorado).

(3) The pilot is then told that the aircraft is 690 miles from Minneapolis, Minnesota. This is the final piece of information needed to determine the aircraft's position. All three circles intersect at only one common point—Denver, Colorado. This is the location of the airplane.

A SIMILAR CONCEPT is used in three-dimensional space, but instead of using intersecting circles to determine position, GPS uses intersecting spheres. The radius of each sphere is determined by the distance of the aircraft from the satellite at the center of each sphere. A reasonably accurate position can be determined using three satellites (or intersecting spheres), but a much more accurate position is provided when using four, and this also provides the pilot with aircraft altitude (distance above sea level). The entire process is performed automatically by a computer within the GPS receiver. The pilot simply observes and uses the results.

GPS NAVIGATION is possible because a GPS receiver computes aircraft position many times per second. By keeping track of aircraft position, the GPS receiver easily calculates aircraft speed over the Earth (groundspeed) and its path (track) relative to the ground.

A panel-mounted GPS receiver with moving-map display.

A handheld GPS receiver with moving-map display.

A GPS DATABASE is similar to the database in smartphones and automobiles that shows cities, highways, and streets. The aviation database, however, contains much more information such as topographical details (the nature of the terrain), rivers and lakes, cities and towns, airports, airways, checkpoints, waypoints, different types of airspace, etc.

A pilot can enter an intended route into the GPS computer, and this route is then shown on the moving-map display. In this manner, the pilot can visually determine if the aircraft is on course or left or right of course. A left–right indicator similar to a VOR course selector is used to remain on the selected GPS course.

A multi-function display (MFD) provides a wide variety of information. The MFD above shows engine instruments, an approach chart to an airport, the route being flown, and a moving-map display.

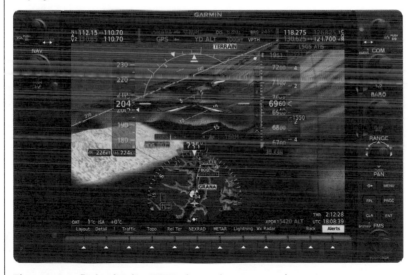

The primary flight display (PFD) above shows primary flight instruments as well as a graphic display of the terrain over which the aircraft is flying.

AN INERTIAL NAVIGATION SYS-TEM (INS) is totally self-contained. It does not need or use radio or satellite signals to determine aircraft position. INS allows a pilot to navigate anywhere in the world using inertia, a property of everything that has mass.

For example, assume that a blindfolded person is seated in the right seat of a stationary automobile. Before getting underway, the driver informs the passenger of their exact location (using geographical coordinates) and the direction in which the automobile is pointed. In other words, the passenger has been programmed with what is needed to keep track of their location.

The driver starts the car and accelerates to 60 mph. Because of its mass (inertia), the passenger's body resists this acceleration, and this resistance is felt as the seat pushes against the passenger's back **(A)**. When the car stops accelerating, the passenger thinks, "Aha. I am now traveling at 60 mph and my internal clock will tell me for how long we will be traveling at this speed and in this direction."

After 30 minutes, the driver slows to 30 mph, a speed change detected by the passenger as her body pitches forward **(B)**. The passenger now knows they traveled for 30 minutes at 60 mph, a distance of 30 miles. Thirty minutes later, the car comes to a screeching halt, and the passenger determines the car has traveled an additional 15 miles for a total of 45 miles.

By carefully keeping track of acceleration, deceleration, and time, the passenger always knows the distance she has traveled. Had the driver turned the car in different directions, the blindfolded

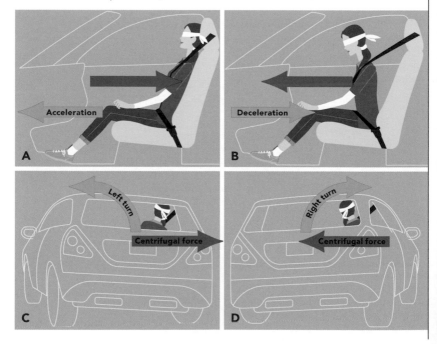

passenger would have been aware of these course changes by the amount (and duration) in which the inertia of her body forces her to lean right **(C)** or left **(D)** during turns due to centrifugal force.

Of course, human beings cannot accurately measure acceleration, keep track of time, and account for all of the minor changes in speed and direction that can occur during even a short ride. This, though, is exactly what an inertial navigation system does. And it does so in three dimensions. The heart of an INS consists of three extremely sensitive accelerometers that measure acceleration in all three planes of aircraft motion: fore and aft, right and left, and up and down. These changes are continuously fed into the INS computer, which continuously converts this information into track and distance

data that is constantly displayed to the pilot on a display unit. The pilot knows where the aircraft is located at all times as well as its current speed and course.

Because INS is oblivious to exterior sources (such as radio waves) and cannot be jammed by an enemy, it found early military acceptance. Germany was first to use inertial navigation when it installed crude guidance systems on its lethal V-2 rockets during World War II. When the preset distance had been traveled by the rocket, a crude onboard computer sent a cutout signal to the rocket engine, and the missile then fell upon its prey in England.

To this day, INS provides a reliable method of navigation and would be especially useful in the event of satellite outages or enemy jamming of GPS signals.

The control panel of an inertial navigation system.

CHAPTER 9
PERFORMANCE

HIGH ELEVATION • WEATHER CONDITIONS • CRUISE CONTROL
AIRCRAFT WEIGHT • AIRCRAFT BALANCE • HUMAN PHYSIOLOGY

HIGH ELEVATION has a dramatic effect on performance. At sea level, a particular light airplane such as a Cessna 172 *(see chart below)* accelerates to takeoff speed in 805 feet. But at an elevation of 7,500 feet, the takeoff distance increases 83 percent to 1,475 feet. Similarly, the climb capability of that airplane diminishes as altitude increases. Also, the distance required to land and brake to a stop is increased at higher elevations.

This decrease in performance is due to air being less dense at high altitudes and elevations than at sea level. For example, the density of air at sea level is typically 0.076 pounds per cubic foot. At 7,500 feet, it is only 0.061 pounds per cubic foot, a reduction of 20 percent. Thin (or less dense) air reduces wing lift and propeller efficiency. Also, aircraft engines produce less power when using air that is less dense than the air at lower altitudes. One benefit of air that is less dense is that it reduces aircraft drag (air resistance).

Typical Performance Data for a Cessna 172

(For example only; do not use for flight planning.)

	Sea level and 59°F (15°C)	2,500 ft and 50°F (10°C)	5,000 ft and 41°F (5°C)	7,500 ft and 32°F (0°C)
Takeoff distance	805 ft	978 ft	1,195 ft	1,475 ft
Takeoff over a 50-ft obstacle	1,400 ft	1,753 ft	2,158 ft	2,717 ft
Landing distance	520 ft	560 ft	603 ft	653 ft
Landing over a 50-ft obstacle	1,250 ft	1,318 ft	1,393 ft	1,478 ft
Rate of climb	770 fpm	652 fpm	535 fpm	415 fpm

WEATHER CONDITIONS also affect aircraft performance. Higher-than-usual temperatures have an adverse effect on performance because hot air is less dense than cold air. For example, air at sea level with a temperature of 104°F (40°C) has the same density as air normally found at 3,000 feet above sea level. Conversely, cold air improves performance. Air at 5,000 feet above sea level with a temperature of −28°F (−33°C) has the same density as air normally found at sea level.

Humidity also decreases performance. Water vapor is lighter than air, and its presence in the atmosphere reduces air density. A reduction in barometric pressure also reduces air density and therefore decreases aircraft performance. An increase in barometric pressure has the opposite effect and is beneficial to performance.

At high temperatures, aircraft performance is reduced and more runway is needed for takeoff and landing.

RUNWAY CONDITIONS affect an airplane's landing performance. Landing on runways coated with snow, rain, or ice requires more stopping distance because there is less friction between the tires and the runway surface. The brakes are less effective. Puddles of water or slush on the runway can hinder takeoff acceleration. Taking off on a grass or dirt runway also decreases takeoff performance and increases takeoff distance. A slippery runway and a crosswind can make ground steering difficult.

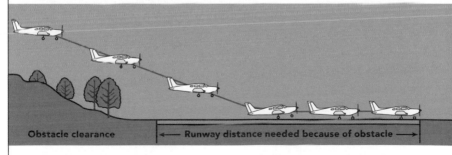

Obstacle clearance ←—— Runway distance needed because of obstacle ——→

An obstacle at the approach (or departure) end of a runway increases the amount of runway needed for landing (or takeoff) because of the space needed to clear the obstacle.

Selected Cruising Data *(For example only; do not use for flight planning.)*

	Speed	Power	Fuel Cons.	Range	Endurance
At 5,000 ft					
Max. speed	142 kt	78%	14.5 gph	770 NM	5.4 hr
Max. range	96 kt	37%	7.3 gph	1,043 NM	10.8 hr
Max. endurance	90 kt	34%	6.8 gph	1,034 NM	11.6 hr
At 15,000 ft					
Max. speed	130 kt	54%	10.4 gph	986 NM	7.6 hr
Max. range	106 kt	40%	7.8 gph	1,078 NM	10.1 hr
Max. endurance	88 kt	34%	6.8 gph	1,021 NM	11.6 hr

CRUISE CONTROL is operating an aircraft so as to obtain the maximum speed, range, or endurance (or a compromise of these goals) at a constant altitude as determined by the purpose of a given flight. The chart above shows selected performance figures used by the pilot of a typical light airplane. At 5,000 feet, for example, 78 percent of its engine's maximum power produces a speed of 142 knots, a fuel consumption of 14.5 gallons per hour, and a range of 770 nautical miles. This airplane can remain aloft under these conditions for 5.4 hours (its endurance).

At 15,000 feet above sea level, the maximum cruising speed is 130 knots, 12 knots slower than at 5,000 feet. This is due to a reduction in engine power at the higher altitude. If strong tailwinds exist at 15,000 feet, the 12-knot loss of airspeed can be more than offset by the increased groundspeed caused by the tailwind. Note that the distance that can be flown (range) is greater at 15,000 feet than at 5,000 feet. One reason for this is the reduced drag (air resistance) at the higher altitude.

The highest altitude to which an airplane can climb is called its *absolute ceiling*. The highest altitude it can reach and still climb 100 feet per minute is its *service ceiling*, a more practical upper limit.

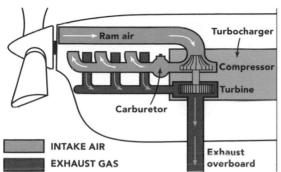

Piston engines lose power at high altitude because there is less oxygen to support combustion. Using a turbocharger (or supercharger) can increase engine power. Driven by the engine's exhaust gases, it pumps pressurized intake air into the engine's induction system.

FOR LONGER DISTANCE, the pilot can operate the airplane at a lower, more efficient speed. In the example shown in the chart on the previous page, at 5,000 feet above sea level, the pilot can fly 1,043 nautical miles at 96 knots while using only 37 percent of the engine's rated power. Although a pilot travels more slowly when flying for distance than when flying for speed, the flight might arrive at its destination sooner because the aircraft might not need to land to refuel along the way.

By using only 34 percent of the engine's power, the pilot can remain aloft for 11.6 hours. Such flying for endurance is done when it is important to conserve fuel, such as when a pilot is lost or needs to circle over an airport (holding) while waiting for the weather to improve. At such times, aircraft speed is unimportant.

INCREASED SPEED can be obtained in a number of ways without using additional engine power. It can be done (1) by polishing the airplane, especially the wings and propeller; (2) by eliminating unnecessary drag (air resistance), such as by realigning a door that does not fit flush with the fuselage; (3) by not carrying heavy loads; and (4) by keeping the engine and aircraft systems properly maintained. An airplane loaded with an aft center of gravity (page 151) flies slightly faster than one loaded with a forward center of gravity.

This airplane has auxiliary, wing tip fuel tanks for increased range.

EXCESS WEIGHT must be eliminated before takeoff. In the specific aircraft scenario described on this page, the pilot must eliminate 87 pounds. There are several options. The pilot can (1) leave behind one passenger or all of the baggage, or (2) drain 87 pounds (14.5 gallons) of fuel from the tanks. This would reduce the available fuel to 27.5 gallons but allow everyone to go along and take all of their baggage. The decreased fuel load, however, might require an enroute fuel stop depending on the length of the proposed flight.

AIRCRAFT WEIGHT must be determined before departure to ensure that it does not exceed the maximum-allowable gross weight specified for the aircraft. An overloaded aircraft is hazardous because it cannot perform properly and is subject to excessive stress and strain on the structure.

One particular four-place airplane, for example, has a maximum-allowable gross weight of 2,300 pounds. Its *empty weight* is 1,370 pounds. This is the weight of the empty airframe and its built-in equipment (e.g., radios). The amount of weight that can be added safely is called the *useful load* and is determined by subtracting the empty weight from the maximum gross weight. In this case, the useful load is 930 pounds.

Aviation fuel weighs 6 pounds per gallon. So if the tanks are full (42 gallons in this example), the total weight of the fuel in the tanks is 252 pounds. Eight quarts of oil in the engine weigh 15 pounds (each gallon of oil weighs 7.5 pounds). The pilot and three passengers in this case weigh 660 pounds, and the baggage weighs 90 pounds. Therefore, the total proposed useful load is 1,017 pounds, which exceeds the maximum allowable 930 pounds by 87 pounds.

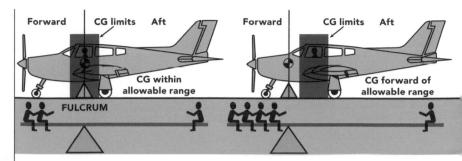

Forward **CG limits** **Aft** — CG within allowable range

Forward **CG limits** **Aft** — CG forward of allowable range

FULCRUM

THE CENTER OF GRAVITY (CG) is determined by the distribution of weight in an aircraft. If a fulcrum were placed beneath the center of gravity, the aircraft would balance like a teeter-totter.

When an airplane is designed, its allowable *CG range* is determined (shown by the red band on the airplanes in the above diagram). An airplane must never be flown when the center of gravity falls outside of these limits. The CG of the aircraft on the left is within limits; it is neither too far forward nor too far aft. The CG of the aircraft on the right is out of limits (out of balance); it is too far forward. Some of the load must be shifted aft to bring the CG within limits.

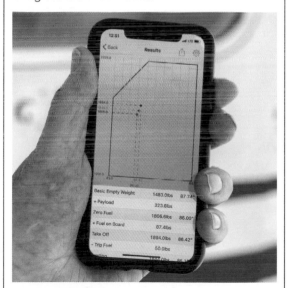

This app is used to solve aircraft weight and balance problems.

WEIGHT AND BALANCE problems are unrelated. The first deals with the amount of weight, and the second deals with where the weight is located. An airplane can have an out-of-limit center of gravity but not be overweight. Also, an airplane can be overloaded but have its CG within limits. If it is determined that an aircraft has an excessively forward or aft CG, the pilot must redistribute the load to bring the airplane within limits.

IMBALANCE can cause undesirable flight characteristics. An excessively forward CG—the airplane is nose heavy—can result in a nose-over tendency, decreased performance, and higher stall speeds. An excessively aft CG—the airplane is tail heavy—can result in dangerous stall characteristics and decreased pitch stability.

HUMAN PHYSIOLOGY affects a person's performance during flight and is as important to safety as aircraft performance. The most common physiological factor that affects a pilot's performance is *hypoxia*. This problem is caused by an insufficient amount of oxygen in the body tissues due to a decrease in the amount of oxygen in the air being breathed. The effects of hypoxia become increasingly problematic as altitude increases above 10,000 feet. Air becomes increasingly less dense, and a given lungful contains less oxygen.

A term often confused for hypoxia is anoxia. Hypoxia is a deficiency of oxygen, whereas anoxia is a total lack of oxygen.

These Air Force pilots are in an altitude chamber used to demonstrate the effects of hypoxia (low oxygen) and hypobaria (low air pressure).

HYPOXIA SYMPTOMS can develop in different sequences and in various forms depending on the rate and duration of climb to altitude, the amount of time spent at altitude, the level of activity or excitement, cockpit temperature, and differences in the individual's health and reactions. Hypoxia usually occurs without noticeable warning and is sometimes accompanied by a false sense of well-being that camouflages the problem.

At 12,000 feet, for example, the effects of hypoxia are present but may be subtle and insidious. Pilots are seldom aware that anything is wrong.

AT HIGHER ALTITUDES (15,000–18,000 feet), the effects of hypoxia on the brain become significant. Muscular control can be impaired, memory can fade intermittently, and a pilot's ability to solve simple problems is impaired.

At 20,000 feet, a pilot might have fits of laughter or crying, impatience, rage, or other emotional disturbances, and significant muscular weakness or, in the extreme, paralysis. Depth perception can become faulty, and double vision can occur. Some pilots feel highly efficient and unaffected even as they approach unconsciousness, while others get sleepy and pass into a stupor.

Above 20,000 feet, most people lose consciousness within a short time.

FOR CONTINUED FLIGHT above 12,500 feet, pilots and passengers in non-pressurized aircraft should use a supplemental source of oxygen. This can be a portable oxygen bottle and masks, or an oxygen system built into the aircraft.

A pressure suit is worn by pilots (and astronauts) who fly so high that the air pressure is too low for an unprotected person to survive.

15 seconds

Lawrence Elliot

35 seconds

Lawrence Elliot

55 seconds

Lawrence Elliot

75 seconds

Lawrence Elliot

95 seconds

Lawrence Elliot

Oxygen supply restored

Lawrence Elliot

In an experiment at an altitude of 25,000 feet, a passenger's oxygen supply was disconnected for 1 minute and 35 seconds. The deterioration of his handwriting shows the rapid effects of hypoxia.

THE RESULTS OF HYPOXIA typically are (1) loss of insight and partial loss of reality; (2) impairment of judgment, inability to think clearly, and a tendency to make errors; (3) a smaller field of vision and decreased hearing; (4) sluggishness and clumsiness; (5) a lack of emotional balance; and (6) significantly reduced vision at night or in dim light.

Deprived of supplemental oxygen at 22,000 feet, a person will remain conscious for only 10 minutes. At 25,000 feet, the time of useful consciousness is only 3 minutes; a person at 40,000 feet will pass out in only 30 seconds and at 60,000 feet will become unconscious in only 12 seconds.

OTHER PROBLEMS are encountered at high altitude because of a decrease in atmospheric pressure. One is the expansion of body gases in the stomach and intestines that

The Mooney M22 Mustang became in 1964 the first pressurized, single-engine airplane.

occurs as atmospheric pressure decreases. At sea level, the stomach contains about a quarter pint of air. At 18,000 feet, this will expand to a half pint and can cause some discomfort but rarely is a serious problem. Relief can be obtained by burping or descending to a lower altitude. Gas-producing foods such as cabbage and carbonated beverages should be avoided before flight, especially if the flight will involve high altitudes.

CONGESTION of the mucous membranes can cause difficulty in maintaining a balance of pressure between the inner ear and the changing atmospheric pressure during climbs and descents. Painful expansion of the inner ear can result. Flying with a head cold should be avoided. The point at which serious discomfort or pain seriously affects a pilot's performance in flight is difficult to predict.

I'M SAFE CHECKLIST

☑ **I**llness—Do I have any symptoms?

☑ **M**edication—Have I been taking prescription or over-the-counter drugs?

☑ **S**tress—Am I under psychological pressure from the job, or am I worried about financial matters, health problems, or family discord?

☑ **A**lcohol—Have I been drinking within 8 hours? Within 24 hours?

☑ **F**atigue—Am I tired and not adequately rested?

☑ **E**motion—Am I emotionally upset?

The I'M SAFE Checklist highlights the elements pilots should use to assess their flight fitness.

CHAPTER 10
WEATHER

CLOUDS • STRUCTURAL ICING • CARBURETOR ICE • THUNDERSTORMS
WEATHER RADAR • RESTRICTED VISIBILITY • WIND • TURBULENCE
THE NATIONAL WEATHER SERVICE

CLOUDS FORM

CLOUDS FORM when air containing sufficient water vapor (an invisible gas) is cooled until the air becomes saturated. The water vapor then condenses to form minute water droplets that are suspended in the air and give the cloud its shape and texture. The same thing happens to moist air surrounding a glass of iced tea. The cold glass cools the air immediately next to the glass, and water vapor in the air condenses to form droplets on the side of the glass.

Have you ever noticed that when compressed gas is allowed to escape from an aerosol can or when air is let out of a tire that the temperature of the escaping gas is considerably colder than the temperature inside the container? This is because when any gas expands (decompresses), its temperature decreases. When air rises in the atmosphere, the atmospheric pressure surrounding it decreases, and the air expands. As a result, it also gets colder.

VISIBILITY is a problem when flying within clouds; it can be virtually zero. A pilot flying in a cloud cannot see the ground or the outside world and, therefore, cannot tell whether the airplane is in a bank, climb, or dive. The pilot must rely on the indications of the instruments to control the airplane's attitude and flight path.

INSTRUMENT FLYING requires a pilot to have special training, skill, and knowledge. An advanced license called an *Instrument Rating* is required for a pilot to fly in cloudiness, and the pilot must also be issued a clearance by air traffic control (to ensure that other aircraft are not flying in the same cloud at the same time). Instrument training may be conducted in an airplane in clear weather. The student wears a special hood *(above)* that allows him or her to see the instruments while blocking the view of outside the airplane. The instructor sits on the right and watches for traffic.

Cloud Chart

Clouds	Symbol	Abbreviation
I. LOW CLOUDS (from the ground to 6,500 ft)		
Stratus: low, uniform sheet cloud	—	St
Stratocumulus: globular masses or rolls	⌄	Sc
II. MIDDLE CLOUDS (6,500–20,000 ft)		
Altostratus: medium-high uniform sheet cloud	∠	As
Nimbostratus: amorphous, rainy layer	⫽	Ns
Altocumulus: sheep-back-like cloud	ω	Ac
III. HIGH CLOUDS (above 20,000 ft)		
Cirrus: thin, featherlike clouds	⌒	Ci
Cirrostratus: very thin, high sheet cloud	2	Cs
Cirrocumulus: thin clouds, cottony or flakelike	⌒ω	Cc
IV. VERTICAL CLOUDS (surface to cirrus layer)		
Cumulus: dense, dome-shaped, puffy	⌂	Cu
Towering cumulus: very tall cumulus	Ⴃ	Cu
Cumulonimbus: thunderstorm, cauliflower towering clouds with cirrus veil on top	⛿	Cb

CLOUDS formed by moist, rising air have a vertical shape and are called *cumulus clouds*. (Cumulus comes from Latin and means "heap.") Air flowing horizontally (wind) is cooled when it travels over colder ground. If the amount of cooling is sufficient, the water vapor in the air condenses and a horizontally shaped *stratus cloud* forms. (Stratus comes from Latin and means "layer.") High *cirrus clouds* form at such cold altitudes that water cannot exist as liquid. These clouds consist of ice crystals. (Cirrus comes from Latin and means "curl.")

Fog is simply a stratus cloud that is less than 50 feet above the ground. It is generally quite shallow. Fog can be a serious problem when it lays a blanket of extremely poor visibility over an airport.

STRUCTURAL ICING is one of the greatest hazards to flying. Below 32°F when water usually freezes, most of the water droplets in a cloud remain in the liquid state because they lack the impurities needed to begin the growth of ice crystals. But when an aircraft flies into these supercooled water droplets, the droplets become unstable and can freeze to the aircraft. A pilot often can get out of an icing zone by descending to an altitude where the air might be warm enough to melt the ice.

CUMULATIVE EFFECTS OF ICE

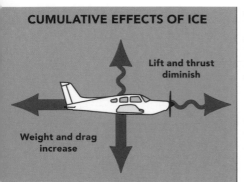

Lift and thrust diminish

Weight and drag increase

AN ACCUMULATION of structural ice on an aircraft has four adverse effects on aircraft performance. It increases aircraft weight (ice weighs 56 pounds per cubic foot); it distorts the shape of the wings, which reduces lift; its bulk and roughness increase drag; and icing on a propeller decreases thrust. One or more of these effects can represent a significant hazard.

CLEAR ICE

Buildup of clear ice on a wing

GLAZE (or CLEAR) ICE forms a transparent coating with a glassy appearance, like the texture of an ice cube. It is more difficult to remove with deice devices. Glaze ice generally forms when flying through cumulus clouds that typically contain large water droplets.

RIME ICE

Buildup of rime ice on a wing

RIME ICE is a white, opaque, granular deposit that usually can be removed more easily. It resembles the ice that can form on the insides of older freezers. Rime ice generally forms when flying through stratiform clouds containing small water droplets.

BLACK DEICING BOOTS (left) are on the leading edges of the wings and vertical and horizontal stabilizers. When ice accumulates on these edges, the boots are turned on and they expand and contract, breaking away the ice.

Alcohol or similar compounds can be sprayed (or slung) onto the leading edges of propellers to prevent ice formation. Also, the leading edges of propellers and wings can be heated to prevent and melt structural ice.

CARBURETOR ICE, unlike structural ice, can occur on a clear day with the outside air temperature as high as 65°F. It forms within the carburetor and chokes the passage through which the fuel-air mixture flows to the engine, causing a power loss. However, it occurs only when the air has a relatively high content of water vapor.

Within the carburetor, fuel and air are mixed proportionately to prepare a volatile mixture that is burned in the engine cylinders. When fuel is added to the air, much of it vaporizes and this causes a drop in temperature. If the temperature in the carburetor drops to 32°F or less, the water vapor can freeze to the carburetor walls.

A LOSS OF POWER can result from carburetor ice, which is initially detected by a slight engine roughness and also can be detected on engine instruments. When the pilot operates the carburetor heat control in the cockpit, the air entering the carburetor is preheated to melt the ice and prevent it from reforming.

THUNDERSTORMS are extremely hazardous. Extreme turbulence can be found anywhere in the storm. Severe updrafts and downdrafts can exceed 60 mph, and flight between them is like flying into a giant pair of scissors that can destroy an aircraft. When downdrafts reach the ground, they spread out horizontally, creating dangerous gusts and wind shifts. Pilots must avoid landing in the vicinity of a thunderstorm.

The chances of hail increase in proportion to storm size. Hailstones have an average diameter of 3/8 inch but can be as large as baseballs, and they can cause heavy structural damage to an airplane. Icing can also be expected in a thunderstorm when flying above the freezing level.

Altimeter errors can be large in the vicinity of a thunderstorm because of rapid pressure changes.

Static electricity (St. Elmo's fire) becomes visible as streaks of bluish fire dancing across the windshield, but it is more dramatic than harmful. It can be reduced in intensity, if desired, by reducing airspeed.

LIGHTNING usually occurs just above the freezing level in a mature thunderstorm. Although an average lightning bolt two miles long has an estimated potential of 25 million volts and a current of 80,000 amperes, it rarely harms an airplane in the air. On the ground, of course, a lightning bolt is dangerous. In the air, lightning can make the aircraft's magnetic compass erratic and hamper some radio reception. Thunder, the noise lightning makes, is seldom heard inside an aircraft.

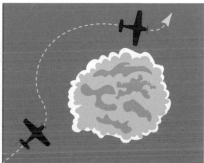

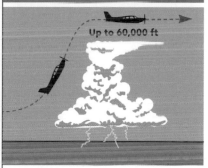

Up to 60,000 ft

IF A THUNDERSTORM IS UNAVOIDABLE, which is highly unlikely, the following rules should be observed when flying through it: (1) Do not fight the updrafts and downdrafts in an attempt to maintain altitude. Ride the currents. (2) Reduce airspeed to reduce stress on the airplane. (3) Use all anti-icing or deicing equipment that is available. (4) Stay at least 4,000 feet above the ground. (5) Try to keep the airplane in a near-level attitude. (6) Turn on cockpit lights to avoid temporary blindness following lightning flashes. (7) Secure loose objects in the cockpit that could be injurious.

TO AVOID A THUNDERSTORM, the best solution is to fly around it at a healthy distance. This may not be possible when approaching a row of storms (a line squall) hundreds of miles long. Flying over the top can be difficult (and turbulent) because the top of a storm can be as high as 60,000 feet (or more). Flying beneath a thunderstorm should be avoided because of the possibility of extreme hail, turbulence, downdrafts that can force an airplane into the ground, and updrafts that can carry an aircraft into the belly of the storm. If a thunderstorm appears unavoidable, land as soon as possible.

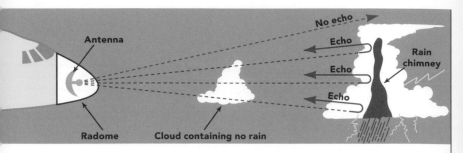

Antenna
No echo
Echo
Rain chimney
Echo
Echo
Radome
Cloud containing no rain

WEATHER RADAR is used to detect thunderstorms and other rain-producing clouds. Pilots say that radar "sees" a storm ahead of the aircraft. The word *see* normally refers to the sensation caused by light striking the retina of the eye, but radar sees differently. A close analogy is found in nature. A blindfolded bat can fly safely through a room of taut, crisscrossed wires. To avoid hitting the wires, the bat emits a series of high-pitched shrieks and listens for the echoes (or *returns*). Thus it determines the direction (and the distance) of an obstacle with respect to its flight path.

Radar works similarly. The radar transmitter sends out a series of high-power radio pulses. These pulses travel ahead of the aircraft in a straight line. If some of them hit a cloud containing rain, the pulses are reflected back to the aircraft. The radar receiver converts these echoes to visual indications on a radar scope.

Intervals of Silence are important. If a bat were to emit a steady shriek interrupted only by brief intervals during which it refilled its lungs, sooner or later the bat would be shrieking when it should be listening. This is why the bat (and the radar transmitter) emit a series of short shrieks (pulses) interlaced with intervals of silence when echoes can be heard.

A flat-plate radar antenna in the nose of a small aircraft, shown with the radome (cover) removed.

USING RADAR is helpful when an aircraft is flying toward a wall of benign clouds beyond which the pilot cannot see. The pilot may elect to fly through the clouds but is concerned about the possibility of thunderstorms that might be hidden behind the wall. The aircraft's radar is used to "see" through the clouds. Some of the radar pulses hit the hidden storms and are reflected back to the receiver.

This Stormscope is showing lightning strikes in the area.

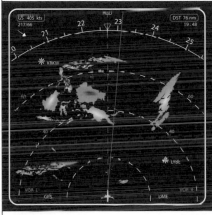

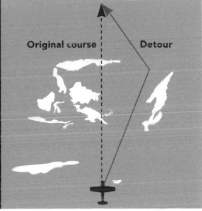

Original course   Detour

ECHOES (rain showers) appear as colored images on the cockpit radar display (light green = least severe, red = most severe). On the screen shown, the arcs, starting with the one at the bottom, represent distances of 20, 40, 60, and 80 miles from the aircraft. A turn to a heading of 240 would be recommended to avoid the red cloud cell shown at a bearing of 220 degrees.

A   **B**   **C**   **D**

THE SHAPE OF AN ECHO is important, too. Fingers (**A**) and hooks (**B**) indicate cyclonic winds radiating from the main portion of the thunderstorm, usually containing hail. A U-shaped pattern (**C**) is a column of hail within a larger area of rain. A scalloped edge (**D**) also is indicative of hail and possible tornadoes.

RESTRICTED VISIBILITY makes it difficult to navigate and to control aircraft attitude visually with respect to the ground.

Haze consists of small particles of dust or other impurities suspended in the air. Much of the reduced visibility near large cities is due to smoke from industrial activities. Haze and smoke combined with fog are erroneously called smog. *Vog* is a visibility restriction resulting from gases and particles from an erupting volcano reacting with oxygen and moisture in the presence of sunlight.

Blowing dust occurs in dry areas when the wind is strong. Wind and vertical currents can spread dust over wide areas, lifting it as high as 15,000 feet.

Sandstorms are more localized than dust storms; sand is seldom lifted more than 100 feet. Visibility within a sandstorm can be near zero. Blowing sand is found in desert regions where loose sand is lifted by strong winds.

Blowing snow occurs when the wind is strong and the fallen snow is fairly dry and light.

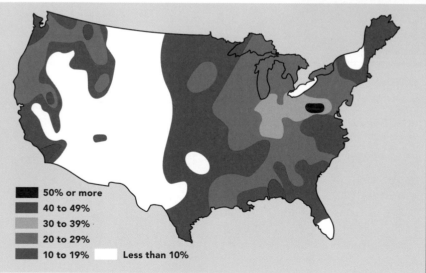

■	50% or more
■	40 to 49%
■	30 to 39%
■	20 to 29%
■	10 to 19% □ Less than 10%

Low visibilities and cloud ceilings prevail more in winter than at any other time. This map shows the percentage of time in winter when the visibility is less than 3 miles and/or the ceiling is less than 1,000 feet.

Poor visibility due to fog at an airport.

A rotating beacon at an airport *(right)* is used at night to help pilots locate the airport and during the day to indicate that the visibility is less than 3 miles and/or the ceiling is less than 1,000 feet above the ground.

Rain seldom reduces visibility below one mile except in brief, heavy showers. However, visibility to the outside of an aircraft can be reduced when rain streams over the windshield or freezes on it.

Precipitation other than rain also can restrict visibility. Drizzle can restrict visibility more than rain because it often is accompanied by fog, haze, or smoke. Heavy snowfall can reduce visibility to near zero.

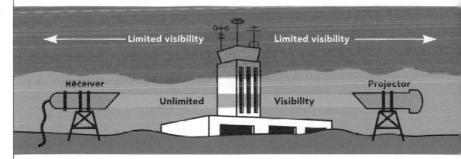

A TRANSMISSOMETER is used to measure the visibility near the touchdown zone of a runway. The visibility in this critical area is frequently different than the visibility observed from the control tower. The unit consists of a projector that sends a beam of light to a receiver. The amount of light received is measured and converted to visibility or *runway visual range* (RVR). During periods of extremely thick fog, no light reaches the receiver, and the RVR for that runway is zero.

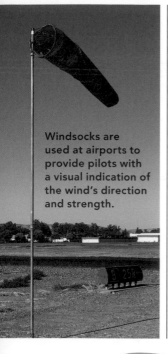

Windsocks are used at airports to provide pilots with a visual indication of the wind's direction and strength.

WIND is the horizontal flow of air. It affects an aircraft's groundspeed, drift, climb angle, and the runway distance required for takeoff and landing. Global wind patterns are highly modified by low- and high-pressure areas that form as a result of the uneven heating of the Earth. One result of this is that winds over the 48 contiguous U.S. states typically blow from west to east (westerly winds).

When a low-pressure area forms, the surrounding higher pressure flows toward and into the low. Because of the Earth's rotation, winds blow clockwise out of a high and counterclockwise into a low in the Northern Hemisphere (and vice-versa in the Southern Hemisphere).

A pilot flying long distance tries to take advantage of wind patterns by flying within those parts of pressure areas where tailwinds (or reduced headwinds) can be found (as long as this does not require flying too far out of the way). The pilot may have to fly a somewhat longer distance to do this, but the tailwinds can actually reduce the time en route.

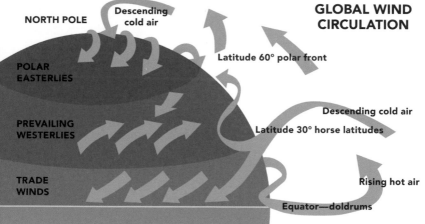

GLOBAL WIND CIRCULATION

NORTH POLE

Descending cold air

Latitude 60° polar front

POLAR EASTERLIES

Descending cold air

PREVAILING WESTERLIES

Latitude 30° horse latitudes

TRADE WINDS

Rising hot air

Equator—doldrums

A GENERAL WIND PATTERN divides each of the Earth's hemispheres into three belts *(above)*. The northeast trade winds occur over the tropics, the prevailing westerlies occur over the mid-latitudes, and the polar easterlies are found between 60 degrees North and the North Pole. The 48 states lie within the belt of westerly winds; pilots flying east most often have a tailwind and those flying west usually have a headwind.

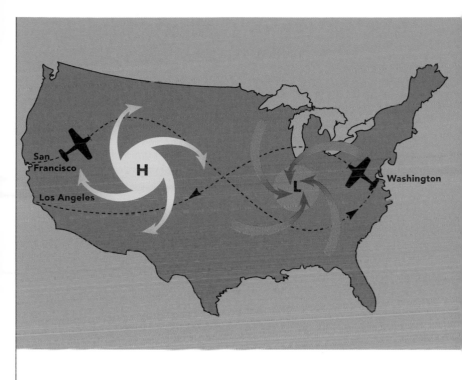

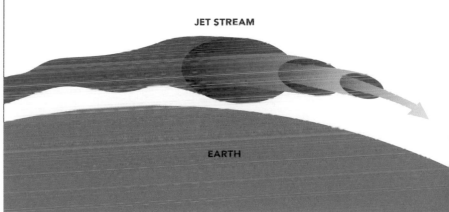

THE JET STREAM is a narrow, shallow, meandering river of high-speed wind that usually extends around the Earth's temperate zone near the top of the troposphere. Wind speeds in a jet stream have been measured at 247 mph but typically are between 100 and 150 mph. The jet stream rarely encircles the Earth as a continuous river of air. It usually is found in segments from 1,000 to 3,000 miles long.

TURBULENCE affecting aircraft ranges all the way from a few annoying bumps to extreme jolts capable of causing structural damage, although extreme turbulence is extremely rare. It is caused by irregular whirls or eddies of air in the atmosphere. The reaction of an aircraft to turbulence varies depending on both the irregular motions of the atmosphere and the characteristics of the aircraft, such as speed, weight, and wing area. Just as when driving fast over a rocky road or speedboating over a choppy lake, reducing speed reduces the effect of turbulence.

MECHANICAL TURBULENCE occurs when air near the ground flows over rough terrain or other obstacles such as tall trees, buildings, and hills. The normally smooth wind flow is transformed into a complicated snarl of eddies similar to rapids in a stream. The degree of turbulence depends on the roughness of the terrain and speed of the wind. This type of turbulence occurs when strong winds blow over steep mountain ridges. The worst turbulence usually is found on the leeward side of a mountain.

TURBULENT CONDITIONS occur when wind blows over steep, sharp mountain ridges. The air on the downwind (leeward) side of the mountain spills chaotically like water rushing down a steep, rocky hill.

Flying over mountainous terrain, such as the Matterhorn (right), provides awe-inspiring views, but strong winds on the leeward side can create teeth-jarring turbulence and perhaps a few uneasy moments.

CONVECTIVE CURRENTS, a major cause of low-altitude turbulence in warm weather, are localized vertical air movements, both ascending and descending. Every rising current has a compensating downward current not far away.

Convective currents develop in air that is heated by contact with a warm surface. Barren areas are warmed faster by the sun than ground covered by vegetation. Thus, uneven heating of the air near the ground causes convective currents to vary in strength.

When cumulus clouds form from moist convective currents, there is rising air beneath and within them. The cloud tops usually represent the upper limit of the convective currents; flight above them is typically smooth.

MECHANICAL TURBULENCE

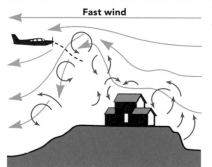

Fast wind

CONVECTIVE TURBULENCE

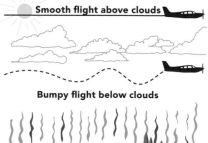

Smooth flight above clouds

Bumpy flight below clouds

Intensity of Turbulence

Light	Occupants may be required to use seat belts; loose objects in the aircraft remain at rest.
Moderate	Occupants are occasionally thrown against their seat belts. Unsecured objects move about.
Severe	The aircraft may be momentarily out of control. Occupants are thrown violently against their seat belts. Unsecured objects are tossed about.
Extreme	The aircraft is tossed about violently and is practically impossible to control. This condition may cause structural damage but is rarely encountered.

WIND SHEAR is an abrupt change in wind speed and/or direction that results in a tearing or shearing effect in the atmosphere. This can produce churning, turbulent air. This band of turbulence typically is narrow, and the degree of turbulence increases as the amount of wind shear increases.

WAKE TURBULENCE contains swirls of air created by the large wings of heavy airplanes disturbing the air and can be quite violent. This invisible threat is especially dangerous to small airplanes taking off or landing closely behind large aircraft, but it can be avoided by giving wake turbulence a few minutes to subside.

WIND-SHEAR TURBULENCE

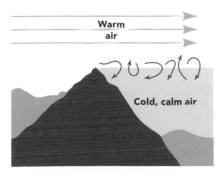

WAKE TURBULENCE

Basic Meteorological and Weather Map Symbols

Haze	∞
Rain	●
Snow	✳
Fog	≡
Drizzle	❚
Smoke	⟿
Showers	▽
Hail	△
Thunderstorm	⊺ĸ
Dust/Sandstorm	⟿
Light turbulence	∧
Moderate turbulence	⋀
Severe Turbulence	⩘
Cold front	▼▼▼▼
Warm front	●●●
Stationary front	▼●▼●
Occluded front	●▲●
Trough	– – –
Ridge	∿∿∿
High/low pressure center (in millibars)	**H**₁₀₃₂ **L**·₉₈₈

A WEATHER BRIEFING is an essential part of flight planning. This pilot is obtaining a self-briefing using a computer at an airport prior to departure. Pilots also can obtain a detailed briefing or a weather update by telephone. En route, pilots should report significant weather changes or unknown flight hazards that could be of value to forecasters and other pilots.

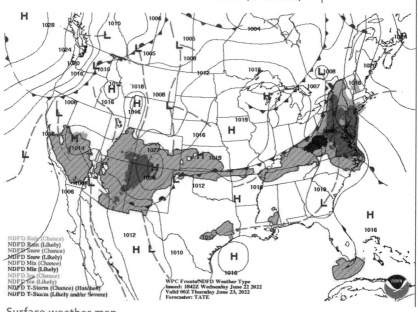

NDFD Rain (Chance)
NDFD Rain (Likely)
NDFD Snow (Chance)
NDFD Snow (Likely)
NDFD Mix (Chance)
NDFD Mix (Likely)
NDFD Ice (Chance)
NDFD Ice (Likely)
NDFD T-Storm (Chance) (Hatched)
NDFD T-Storm (Likely and/or Severe)

WPC Fronts/NDFD Weather Type
Issued: 1842Z Wednesday June 22 2022
Valid 00Z Thursday June 23, 2022
Forecaster: TATE

Surface weather map.

THE NATIONAL WEATHER SERVICE gathers weather data from all over the world, prepares reports and forecasts, and distributes them where needed.

- *METARs* (Aviation Routine Weather Reports), issued hourly, provide the current weather conditions at most airports. A sample METAR is decoded below. Special reports are issued when the weather changes significantly between hourly reports.
- *TAFs* (Terminal Area Forecasts) are issued every 6 hours and cover a 24- or 30-hour period.
- *Winds and temperatures aloft forecasts* provide the wind direction, wind speed, and temperature for various altitudes at various locations and are important in flight planning.
- *SIGMETs* are special advisories when necessary to warn pilots of significant and hazardous weather conditions that could affect the safety of all aircraft, such as severe turbulence, severe icing conditions, thunderstorms, and volcanic ash.
- *AIRMETs* are other special advisories that warn of less severe conditions such as moderate turbulence and icing, surface winds of 30 knots or more, and extensive areas of cloudiness and low visibility.
- *PIREPs* (pilot reports) are weather conditions observed and reported by pilots that are distributed to other pilots who might not be aware of such conditions.
- A wide variety of graphical charts provide a plethora of weather information. These include surface (ground) analysis charts, significant weather charts, prognostic (forecast) charts, atmospheric pressure patterns, etc.

METAR KRNT 221853Z 35006KT 5SM BR OVC008 16/14 A3017 RMK AO2 CIG 005V011 SLP222 T01560139

METAR	Explanation[1]	Example
KRNT	ICAO location indicator	KRNT = Renton Municipal Airport
221853Z	Date and time of report (2-digit day of the month + 4 digit time in UTC [Zulu])	22nd of the month; 18:53 Zulu
35006KT	Wind conditions (3-digit direction to nearest 10°); speed (2–3 digits)	Winds from the North (350°) at 6 knots (7 mph, 3.1 m/s)
5SM	Visibility in U.S. statute miles (SM)	Visibility = 5 SM (8 km)
BR	Weather (e.g., BR = mist, FG = fog, GR = hail, RA = rain, TS = thunderstorm, etc.)	Mist
OVC008	Cloud amount (OVC = overcast), 3-digit height (100s of feet), and type	Overcast cloud deck at 800 feet AGL
16/14	2-digit temp/dew point (°C)	Temp 16°C; dew point 14°C
A3017	Pressure (altimeter)—inches and hundredths	Pressure 30.17 inches Hg
RMK AO2	Remarks: type of automated station	A02 = with precipitation
CIG 005V011	Ceiling (lowest–highest, 100s of feet)	Ceiling varying, 500–1,100 feet
SLP222	Sea-level pressure (in hectopascals)	Sea-level pressure 1022.2 hPa
T01560139	Temp and dew point (tenths of °C)	Temp 15.6°C, dew point 13.9°C

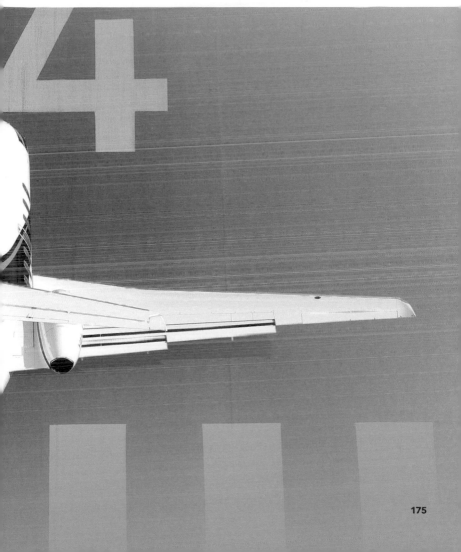

CHAPTER 11
AIRPORTS AND AIR TRAFFIC CONTROL

RADIO COMMUNICATIONS • THE CONTROL TOWER • AIRPORTS
TRAFFIC SEPARATION • FLIGHT SERVICE STATIONS • EMERGENCIES
CONVERTING MEASUREMENTS

A pilot calls ground control for clearance to taxi.

A panel-mounted GPS incorporates a transceiver.

RADIO COMMUNICATIONS are a pilot's invisible link with the ground. Two-way radio allows pilots to obtain information and assistance from a variety of ground stations and from other aircraft. The typical aircraft communications radio is called a *transceiver* because it combines a transmitter and a receiver. Many aircraft have more than one transceiver, which is like a telephone in that a pilot can speak and listen, but with a transceiver, the pilot cannot do both at the same instant.

Most air-to-ground communications are done using very-high frequency (VHF) transceivers on frequencies that range from 118 to 136 MHz. Long-range communications are accomplished using either high-frequency (HF) or satellite transceivers. Before transmitting, a pilot ensures that the aircraft's transceiver is tuned to the proper frequency (usually obtained from an aeronautical chart) and that no one else is talking. After planning what to say, the pilot holds the microphone close to his or her mouth (when using a handheld microphone), depresses the transmitter button, and speaks in a normal tone of voice.

Although the message may be phrased in a pilot's own words, specific words and phrases are commonly used to reduce the length of radio transmissions and provide some uniformity. Some of the ones most commonly used are shown on the next page.

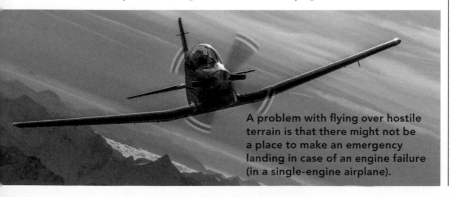

A problem with flying over hostile terrain is that there might not be a place to make an emergency landing in case of an engine failure (in a single-engine airplane).

WHEN LISTENING to an aircraft radio, it is sometimes easy to misinterpret what is being said. For example, the letters B, D, P, V and T can sound very much alike, especially when radio reception is poor. The same is true of F and S. To avoid confusion, pilots use the phonetic alphabet (right) instead of using individual letters. You can also spell a word using the phonetic alphabet. For example, the word "pilot" can be transmitted or spoken as "papa, india, lima, oscar, tango." Note that there also are phonetic pronunciation guides for the numbers 0 through 9.

Standard Radio Phraseology

Phrase	Meaning
Read back	Repeat all of this message back to me.
Roger	I have received all of your last message.
Say again	(self-explanatory)
Speak slower	(self-explanatory)
Stand by	I must pause for a few seconds.
That is correct	(self-explanatory)
Verify	Check with originator.
Mayday	International distress signal.
Acknowledge	Let me know that you have received and understand this message.
Affirmative	Yes.
Correction	An error has been made in this transmission. The correct version is…
Go ahead	Proceed with your message.
I say again	(self-explanatory)
Negative	No.
Out	The conversation is ended; no response needed.
Over	My transmission is ended; I expect a response.
How do you read	Can you hear my transmissions clearly?
Wilco	I understand message and will comply.
Words twice	Communications are difficult; please say every word/group of words twice.
Unable	Cannot comply.

Phonetic Alphabet

A	Alpha
B	Bravo
C	Charlie
D	Delta
E	Echo
F	Foxtrot
G	Golf
H	Hotel
I	India
J	Juliet
K	Kilo
L	Lima
M	Mike
N	November
O	Oscar
P	Papa
Q	Quebec
R	Romeo
S	Sierra
T	Tango
U	Uniform
V	Victor
W	Whiskey
X	X-ray
Y	Yankee
Z	Zulu
0	Zee-ro
1	Wun
2	Too
3	Tree
4	Fow-er
5	Fife
6	Six
7	Sev-en
8	Ait
9	Nin-er

WHEN READY TO DEPART, a pilot calls ground control for permission to taxi. The controller then advises the pilot which route to take to get to the runway in use. When near the runway and ready for takeoff, the pilot tunes to the tower frequency and advises the controller that he is "ready for takeoff." When traffic conditions permit, the pilot is "cleared for takeoff."

LANDING SEQUENCE is established once the aircraft is in the traffic pattern. The pilot is advised which other aircraft to follow and is informed of other aircraft in the immediate vicinity. After landing, the pilot taxis off the runway and contacts ground control on another frequency. This controller directs the pilot to the destination on the airport and often will advise of possible hazards such as ditches, construction areas, and so forth.

CONTROL TOWER operators are air traffic controllers responsible for directing aircraft on the ground and those flying in the vicinity of the airport. They especially ensure that there is only one aircraft on a runway (taking off or landing) at a time.

Most airports do not have control towers because there is not enough traffic to justify the cost. Aircraft flying in and out of these *nontowered airports* use the "see and be seen" method of traffic separation. In other words, they communicate with each other by radio and look out for each other.

A pilot intending to land at a *towered airport* first tunes to a special radio frequency to listen to a recording that provides the runway in use, weather conditions, wind speed and direction, and other information regarding the airport. The pilot then contacts the control tower by radio before entering the traffic area. The tower operator then gives the pilot permission to enter the traffic pattern.

RADAR is available at major airports and is used by *approach controllers* and *departure controllers* to assist in directing aircraft to and from the airport, especially during periods of bad weather. Most aircraft are equipped with transponders, electronic devices that better enable radar controllers to determine the identification, position, and altitude of the aircraft under their control. A newer system called ADS-B (Automatic Dependent Surveillance–Broadcast) provides controllers with even more exacting information about the position of aircraft. This is because ADS-B equipped aircraft continuously broadcast their GPS (satellite navigation) positions to air traffic controllers. ADS-B also broadcasts a pilot's position to other aircraft so that pilots can more easily avoid conflict with one another.

Type of light signal		Aircraft on ground	Aircraft in air
Steady green		Cleared for takeoff	Cleared to land
Flashing green		Cleared to taxi	Return for landing
Steady red		Stop	Give way to other aircraft and circle airport
Flashing red		Taxi clear of runway	Airport unsafe—do not land
Flashing white		Return to starting point on airport	N/A
Alternating red and green		General warning signal: Exercise extreme caution	

LIGHT SIGNALS are used at an airport when radio communication fails. A pilot can receive instructions from the control tower by interpreting light signals flashed toward the aircraft. Refer to the table of light signals above. The tower controller sends the general warning signal when the pilot needs to be alerted about a particular hazard. For example, the pilot might have forgotten to lower the aircraft's landing gear.

AIRPORTS come in all sizes and shapes. Some are large complexes with numerous long, concrete runways that are more than two miles long. Most, however, like the one below, have only one or two hard-surface runways a few thousand feet long. Others can be short dirt or grass strips carved from the wilderness. *Seaports* are designated areas of water on rivers or lakes that are used by seaplanes. *Heliports* are small areas not much larger in area than the helicopters that use them.

A runway is numbered according to its magnetic direction. The direction is rounded off to the nearest 10 degrees and the last digit is dropped. For example, the runway in the diagram on the next page is aligned east (090°) and west (270°). It is numbered 9 and 27, depending upon the direction of takeoff and landing. If an airport has two parallel runways, they might be labeled 9L (for the left runway) and 9R (for the right runway). When operating in the opposite direction, they would be labeled 27R and 27L. When there are three parallel runways, the center runway usually is labeled with a "C" (e.g., 9C and 27C).

A TRAFFIC PATTERN *(right)* is established to provide an organized flow of traffic about an airport. The standard traffic pattern in the United States is a left-hand pattern; the flow of traffic is counterclockwise. A right-hand (clockwise) pattern is used only when a left-hand pattern is impractical, such as when a portion of such a pattern would extend over a housing development. Using a right-hand pattern then places traffic on the other side of the airport and eliminates noise for those living under a left-hand pattern. The standard altitude at which airplanes fly in the traffic pattern varies from 600 to 1,500 feet above the airport elevation, but 1,000 feet is most common and the altitude depends on local conditions and regulations. (The pattern altitude for military jets can be as high as 2,500 feet.)

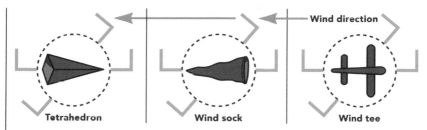

Wind direction

Tetrahedron   Wind sock   Wind tee

A WIND INDICATOR, enclosed in a large, segmented circle, is displayed at most airports. The three common types above, for example, show the wind blowing from the east, indicating that takeoffs and landings should be made on Runway 9 (into the wind and toward the east). The L-shaped indicators show that the use of Runway 9 requires a left-hand traffic pattern. When the wind blows from the west, pilots use Runway 27 and fly a right-hand pattern. A northeast wind would indicate use of Runway 4, and so forth. Sometimes the wind "splits" the runways, and the pilot has a choice of which one to use.

WHEN DEPARTING from an airport without a control tower, the pilot looks at the wind indicator to determine which runway and what type of traffic pattern to use. The pilot taxis to the runway and, when ready for takeoff, visually scans the vicinity of the airport to see that no one is about to land.

UPON ARRIVING at an airport without a control tower, the pilot flies over the airport at least 1,000 feet above traffic pattern altitude to look at the wind indicator and determine which runway and what type of traffic pattern to use. The pilot then flies away from the area, descends to pattern altitude, and enters the flow of traffic at a 45-degree angle to the runway (see diagram below).

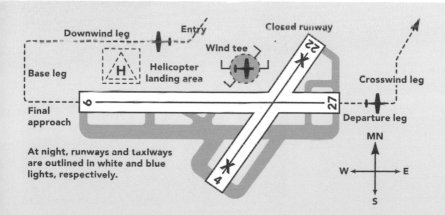

Downwind leg   Entry   Closed runway

Wind tee

Base leg   H   Helicopter landing area

Final approach   6   27   Crosswind leg

Departure leg

At night, runways and taxiways are outlined in white and blue lights, respectively.

MN

W — E

S

LARGE INTERNATIONAL AIRPORTS can look from above like complex spider webs of runways, taxiways, ramps, and terminal buildings. Some are as large as small cities. Chicago's O'Hare International Airport *(below)* has eight runways that total more than 74,000 feet in length. The world's busiest airport (in terms of passenger use) has consistently been the Hartsfield-Jackson International Airport in Atlanta, Georgia. The world's largest airport (in square miles) is Saudi Arabia's King Fahd International Airport.

Every airport has a unique three-letter location identifier. For example, pilots refer to Los Angeles International Airport as LAX, Seattle-Tacoma International Airport as SEA, and John F. Kennedy International Airport (serving New York City) as JFK. Airport identifiers in the contiguous United States are preceded by the letter K, such as KLAX, KSEA, KJFK, and so forth.

Pilots use airport diagrams to keep track of their position on the airport, keep their aircraft clear of conflict with other aircraft, and prevent them from crossing active runways without permission, a safety hazard called a runway incursion.

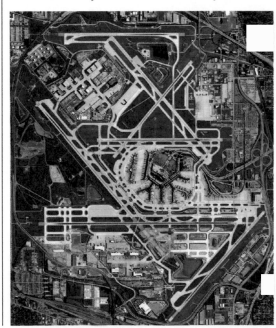

Airport Signs and Markings

Type of Sign and Meaning		Type of Marking and Meaning	
`15-33`	**Runway Holding Position**—Hold short of intersecting runway		**Holding Position**—Hold short of intersecting runway
`15-APCH`	**Runway Approach Holding Position**—Hold short of aircraft on approach to runway		**ILS Critical Area/POFZ Boundary**—Hold short when instructed by ATC
`ILS`	**ILS Critical Area Holding Position**—Hold short of ILS approach critical area		**Taxiway/Taxiway Holding**—Hold short of intersecting taxiway
`⊖`	**No Entry**—Aircraft entry is prohibited		**Non-Movement Area Boundary**—Denotes boundary between movement area and non-movement area
`T`	**Taxiway Location**—Identifies taxiway on which the aircraft is located		
`15`	**Runway Location**—Identifies runway on which the aircraft is located		**Taxiway Edge (solid)**—Defines edge of usable, full-strength taxiway (adjoining pavement not usable)
`3`	**Runway distance remaining**—The length (in 1000s of feet) of runway remaining.		
	Runway boundary—Exit boundary from runway protected area		**Taxiway Edge (dashed)**—Defines edge of taxiway where adjoining pavement is usable
	ILS critical area boundary—Exit boundary of ILS critical area		
`J→`	**Taxiway Direction**—Defines designation and direction of intersecting taxiway		
`↖L`	**Runway Exit**—Defines designation and direction of exit taxiway from runway		
`22↑`	**Outbound Destination**—Defines directions to take-off runways		
`FBO↘`	**Inbound Destination**—Directs arriving aircraft to airport destinations		
NOISE ABATEMENT PROCEDURES IN EFFECT 2200 0600	**Information**—Provides procedural or other specialized information		
	Taxiway Ending Marker—Taxiway does not continue beyond intersection		

This sign indicates that the pilot is on Taxiway D (Delta) and is about to cross Taxiway B (Bravo).

TRAFFIC SEPARATION is critical for safety. Pilots flying in clear weather and using visual flight rules (VFR) avoid conflict with other aircraft by visual observation and, when necessary, deviate from course. Pilots flying in cloudiness and using instrument flight rules (IFR) cannot see other aircraft. They communicate with air traffic control (ATC) personnel, called *controllers*, who provide safe separation between aircraft.

Prior to departure, a pilot receives an ATC clearance providing authorization to fly along a prescribed route at a specified altitude. This assures that the pilot will be provided a large block of surrounding airspace in which no other aircraft will be allowed to fly.

A typical ATC clearance received by radio prior to departure might go something like this:

Cessna 3456B cleared to Paso Robles airport via Gaviota, Victor 27 to Morro Bay, direct. Climb and maintain two thousand, expect eight thousand one zero minutes after departure. Departure frequency 119.05, squawk 4576.

This clearance is copied (written down) by the pilot using a special shorthand, as shown below.

C/PRB
GVO V27 MQO DIR
2,000 / 8,000 - 10
119.05 4576

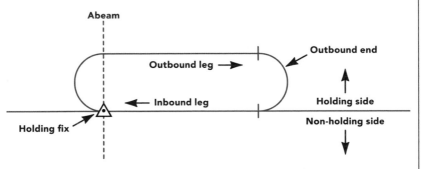

A HOLDING PATTERN is an air traffic controller's "red light," a way to prevent a pilot from progressing any farther along his or her route. This might be because of air-traffic congestion, conflicting traffic, weather delays, or other reasons. A pilot obviously cannot pull over and stop, so the pilot is directed to *hold* at a specific navigational fix and altitude along the route. The standard holding pattern *(above)* uses right-hand turns in a racetrack-shaped pattern, and each complete pattern takes four minutes to complete.

A nonstandard holding pattern, which requires turning to the left, is used only when specified in the ATC clearance instructions or depicted on the chart. A nonstandard holding pattern might have unusually long legs and would take longer to complete than a standard pattern.

Pilots must be cautious, however, about allowing their aircraft to be held for too long when and if their fuel supply becomes a concern. At such a time, they must advise the controller that it would be unsafe for them to continue holding beyond a certain time.

Aircraft flying along airways in the United States are observed by air traffic controllers because of remotely located radar and ADS-B sites that constantly monitor the skies. After takeoff, the pilot contacts an air traffic controller who identifies the aircraft on the ATC display and keeps track of its altitude and progress.

When flying a route that might not be observable to a controller, pilots intermittently report their position and altitude at designated points. A typical position report is as follows:

Los Angeles Center, this is Cessna six-seven-seven-two-sierra, Perch Intersection, at zero-niner-one-zero [time], maintaining 7,000 [altitude]. Estimating Squid [next checkpoint] at zero-niner-two six, Kwang [checkpoint after next]. Over.

AIR ROUTE TRAFFIC CONTROL CENTERS

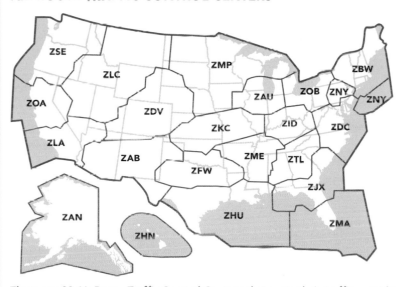

There are 22 Air Route Traffic Control Centers that control air traffic over the 50 U.S. states. One of the smallest and busiest is Chicago Center (ZAU).

ZSE—Seattle Center	ZMP—Minneapolis Center	ZBW—Boston Center
ZOA—Oakland Center	ZAU—Chicago Center	ZNY—New York Center
ZLC—Salt Lake City Center	ZKC—Kansas City Center	ZID—Indianapolis Center
ZDV—Denver Center	ZFW—Fort Worth Center	ZDC—Washington D.C. Center
ZLA—Los Angeles Center	ZHU—Houston Center	ZTL—Atlanta Center
ZAB—Albuquerque Center	ZME—Memphis Center	ZJX—Jacksonville Center
ZAN—Anchorage Center	ZOB—Cleveland Center	ZMA—Miami Center
ZHN—Honolulu Center		

FLIGHT SERVICE STATIONS (FSS) are called or visited prior to a flight away from a local airport. The pilot is briefed about the weather and wind along the planned route of flight and receives appropriate weather forecasts. The pilot is also advised about the status of navigational aids along the route (some might be off the air), the condition of the destination airport (the runways might be covered with snow and ice, or one might be closed for other reasons), and so forth. This information also may be obtained online.

After receiving a prefight briefing, the pilot then files a flight plan that lists the type of aircraft being flown, its speed, registration number, color, fuel supply, number of passengers aboard, estimated time of departure (ETD), proposed route and altitude, estimated time en route (ETE), and pilot's name and contact information. While en route, a pilot should use the aircraft's radio to report a change in the route or estimated time of arrival (ETA).

If the pilot fails to file an arrival report within one hour after the ETA, a local search is begun. If the pilot is not located within the next two hours, a full-scale search-and-rescue operation is begun.

In the case of an in-flight emergency, three of the pilot's primary responsibilities are to (1) AVIATE (control the airplane), (2) NAVIGATE (fly the aircraft in a safe direction), and (3) COMMUNICATE (the dilemma to a nearby air traffic control facility for assistance). An air traffic control facility also can provide assistance should the pilot become lost or disoriented. At such a time, the pilot should consider abiding by the Five Cs: CONFESS the problem, COMMUNICATE all available and pertinent information, CONFORM to instructions from a controller, CLIMB to a higher altitude to improve radio communications, and CONSERVE fuel by operating the engine at reduced power.

If a pilot is forced down, the appropriate distress signals (*right*) should be laid out on the ground to inform search-and-rescue aircraft of the situation. This can be done with large strips of fabric, pieces of wood, stones, or other items. If the search aircraft is circling low enough, a pilot can transmit signals (*below*) with his or her body.

VISUAL EMERGENCY SIGNALS

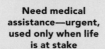

Need medical assistance—urgent, used only when life is at stake

Can proceed shortly—wait if practical

Need mechanical help or parts— long delay

All OK—do not wait

Do not attempt to land here

A pilot is not required to file a flight plan (in the U.S.) but should do so because it is a form of free insurance. Otherwise, in the unlikely event of a forced landing en route, no one would know that the pilot is missing and along which route to search.

A danger when flying over large bodies of water in a single-engine airplane is that the pilot might have to make a water landing (a ditching) in the event of an engine failure.

Ground-to-Air Emergency Code Distress Signals

I	Require doctor, serious injuries	¦	Require signal lamp with battery, and radio	L	Require fuel and oil
I I	Require medical supplies	K	Indicate direction to proceed	LL	All well
X	Unable to proceed	↑	Am proceeding in this direction	N	No
F	Require food and water	I>	Will attempt takeoff	Y	Yes
⩔	Require firearms and ammunition	L⌐	Aircraft seriously damaged	JL	Not understood
☐	Require map and compass	△	Probably safe to land here	W	Require mechanic

If in doubt, use international symbol: ⊐ ☐ ⊏

Land here	Use drop message	Our receiver is operating	Negative (NO)	Affirmative (YES)	Pick us up—plane abandoned

CONVERTING MEASUREMENTS from one system to another is sometimes necessary, especially when pilots fly from one country to another. For example, many countries use the metric system and express all temperatures in degrees Celsius. In a few countries, altitude is designated in meters, and many specify distances in kilometers. It can be confusing to U.S. pilots when climb rate is expressed in meters per second and volume (usually of fuel) is measured in imperial gallons or liters. Pilots might also have to deal with atmospheric pressure expressed in millibars and weight in kilograms. At such times, the following tables can be handy.

Weight

Pounds	Kilograms
1.0 lb	0.45 kg
2.0 lb	0.91 kg
2.2 lb	1.0 kg
3.0 lb	1.36 kg
4.0 lb	1.81 kg
4.4 lb	2.0 kg
5.0 lb	2.27 kg
11.0 lb	5.0 kg
15.0 lb	6.8 kg
33.1 lb	15.0 kg

Distance

Statute Mile	Nautical Mile	Kilometer
0.62 SM	0.54 NM	1.0 km
1.0 SM	0.87 NM	1.61 km
1.15 SM	1.0 NM	1.85 km
3.11 SM	2.7 NM	5.0 km
5.0 SM	4.35 NM	8.05 km
5.76 SM	5.0 NM	9.27 km
9.32 SM	8.09 NM	15.0 km
15.0 SM	13.03 NM	24.14 km
17.28 SM	15.0 NM	27.79 km
200.0 SM	173.8 NM	321.9 km

Volume

U.S. Gallon	Imperial Gallon	Liter
0.3 gal	0.2 gal	1.1 l
1.0 gal	0.8 gal	3.8 l
1.2 gal	1.0 gal	4.6 l
1.3 gal	1.1 gal	4.9 l
4.0 gal	3.3 gal	15.0 l
5.0 gal	4.2 gal	19.0 l
6.0 gal	5.0 gal	22.7 l
15.0 gal	12.5 gal	56.8 l
18.0 gal	15.0 gal	68.1 l
20.0 gal	16.7 gal	75.7 l

Temperature

Fahrenheit	Celsius
120°F	49°C
100°F	38°C
80°F	27°C
60°F	16°C
40°F	5°C
32°F	0°C
20°F	−7°C
0°F	−18°C
−20°F	−29°C
−40°F	−40°C

Altitude

Feet	Meters
1.0 ft	0.3 m
3.3 ft	1.0 m
5.0 ft	1.5 m
100 ft	30.5 m
328 ft	100 m
500 ft	152 m
1,000 ft	305 m
1,640 ft	500 m
5,000 ft	1,524 m
16,400 ft	5,000 m

Pressure

Inches of Mercury	Millibars
1.0 in	34 mb
20.00 in	677 mb
25.00 in	847 mb
26.00 in	881 mb
27.00 in	914 mb
28.00 in	948 mb
29.00 in	982 mb
29.92 in	1013 mb
30.00 in	1016 mb
31.00 in	1050 mb

This airplane has a groundspeed of 360 kilometers per hour, has 62 liters of fuel remaining in its fuel tanks, is climbing slowly (3 meters per second) to an altitude of 3,048 meters, and is carrying 18 kilograms in the baggage compartment. The altimeter setting is 997 millibars and the outside air temperature is 1°C. U.S. pilots flying overseas often need to be familiar with these units.

TIME CONVERSIONS are necessary because an airplane's speed can carry it across several time zones during a lengthy flight. Instead of adapting to changing time zones, pilots use Coordinated Universal Time (UTC), which also is known as Greenwich Mean Time (GMT), no matter where they are in the world. UTC (or GMT) is the local standard time at Greenwich, England. It was chosen as a standard for the world because Greenwich lies on the Earth's prime meridian (0° longitude). The table below shows the conversions of local time to and from UTC in U.S. time zones. For example, when it is 3:15 a.m. local time in Los Angeles (Pacific Standard Time), UTC is determined by adding 8 hours, resulting in 11:15 a.m.

To Change UTC to Local Time	Time Zone	To Change Local Time to UTC
Subtract 4 hours	Eastern Daylight	Add 4 hours
Subtract 5 hours	Eastern Standard	Add 5 hours
Subtract 5 hours	Central Daylight	Add 5 hours
Subtract 6 hours	Central Standard	Add 6 hours
Subtract 6 hours	Mountain Daylight	Add 6 hours
Subtract 7 hours	Mountain Standard	Add 7 hours
Subtract 7 hours	Pacific Daylight	Add 7 hours
Subtract 8 hours	Pacific Standard	Add 8 hours
Subtract 9 hours	Alaska Standard	Add 9 hours
Subtract 10 hours	Hawaii-Aleutian Standard	Add 10 hours
Subtract 11 hours	Bering Standard	Add 11 hours

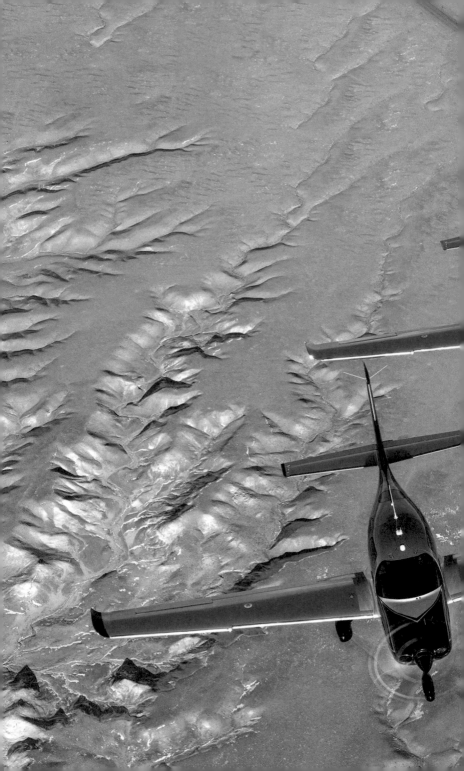

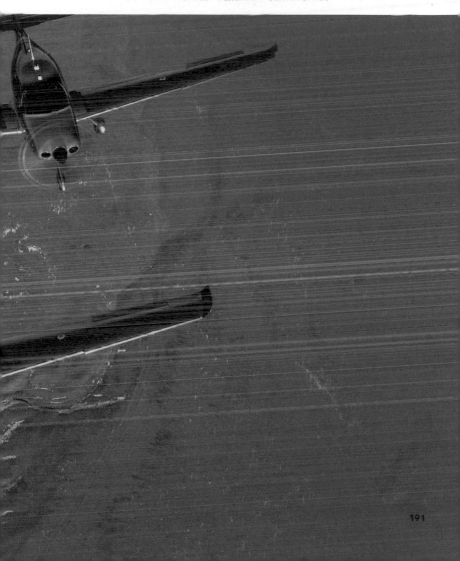

CHAPTER 12
AVIATION REGULATIONS

REGULATIONS GOVERNING FLYING • MINIMUM SAFE ALTITUDES
POSITION LIGHTS • PILOT RESPONSIBILITIES • STUDENT PILOTS
PILOT CERTIFICATES • AIRCRAFT CERTIFICATES

FORMATION FLYING is prohibited except by prior arrangement between each of the pilots involved. Flying near other aircraft is prohibited when the closeness creates a collision hazard. The minimum safe distance between two aircraft in formation depends on pilot skill and the maneuverability of the aircraft.

THE REGULATIONS GOVERNING FLYING are numerous and frequently complex. Some are difficult to translate into everyday language. Consequently, some generalizations are required in explaining the following examples of aviation regulations. They are not to be considered as legal authority.

RIGHT OF WAY over all other aircraft is reserved for an aircraft in distress. When two aircraft of the same category are converging at the same altitude (except head-on), the aircraft at the other's right has the right of way **(A)**. If aircraft of different categories are converging, a balloon has right of way over all other aircraft; a glider has right of way over an airship, airplane, or rotorcraft; and an airship has right of way over an airplane or rotorcraft.

When two aircraft approach each other head-on, each pilot shall alter course to the right **(B)**. An aircraft being overtaken has the right of way, and the overtaking aircraft shall pass on the right and well clear of the other **(C)**. When two airplanes approach an airport to land, the airplane at the lower altitude has the right of way **(D)**.

There are times, however, when exercising right of way might be not only impractical but also dangerous. For example, if a light aircraft pilot has right of way over a Boeing 747 jumbo jet, prudence and common sense dictate that the pilot should exercise courtesy (and discretion) and yield to the airliner.

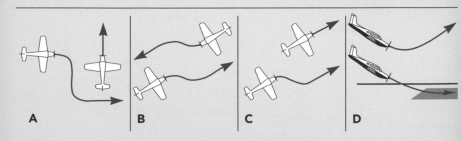

A   B   C   D

VISUAL FLIGHT RULES (VFR) state what minimum weather conditions must exist for a pilot to fly legally. In order to fly in poor (or lesser) conditions, pilots must learn to fly by instruments and obtain an Instrument Rating, a license required to fly in inclement weather. This allows pilots to fly legally in a wide variety of weather conditions, although they must abide by instrument flight rules (IFR).

The minimum visibility required to fly VFR in controlled airspace is 3 miles. Outside of controlled airspace, it is 1 mile. The minimum flight visibility is 5 miles when flying above 10,000 feet.

A pilot may not take off, land, or enter the traffic pattern of an airport in controlled airspace unless the cloud ceiling (cloud base) is at least 1,000 feet above the ground and the visibility is at least 3 miles.

A pilot flying VFR outside of controlled airspace may fly as close to clouds as safety allows but must always remain clear of the clouds.

Within controlled airspace, pilots must maintain minimum distances from all clouds (as shown below), depending on whether they are flying over, under, or around the clouds.

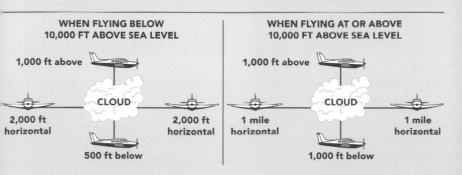

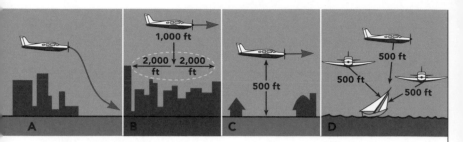

MINIMUM SAFE ALTITUDES must be maintained by a pilot except when taking off or landing. The following rules were established to provide safe operating conditions for the pilot and passengers as well as safety for people and property on the ground. **(A)** A pilot must fly high enough so that in case of an engine failure, the aircraft can glide to an area that allows a safe emergency landing to be made without creating a hazard to persons or property on the ground. **(B)** When flying over congested areas (cities, towns, open-air assemblies), the pilot of an airplane must fly at least 1,000 feet above the highest obstacle (such as a high-rise building or radio tower) that is within a 2,000-foot horizontal distance of the aircraft. **(C)** When flying over other-than-congested areas, a pilot must fly at least 500 feet above the ground. **(D)** When flying over open water or sparsely populated areas, the aircraft may not be operated closer than 500 feet (in any direction) to any person, boat, vehicle, or structure.

Helicopters, powered parachutes, and weight-control aircraft may be flown at altitudes below those stated above.

CRUISING ALTITUDES were established to prevent aircraft that are flying in opposite directions from flying at the same altitude. When flying in a generally easterly direction (000° to 179°), pilots flying in accordance with visual flight rules (VFR) must fly at an odd-thousand-foot altitude plus 500 feet (5,500 feet, 7,500 feet, 9,500 feet, etc.). When flying in a generally westerly direction (180° to 359°), pilots must fly at an even-thousand-foot altitude plus 500 feet (4,500 feet, 6,500 feet, 8,500 feet, etc.).

POSITION LIGHTS are required to be turned on when flying at night (from sunset to sunrise). These lights consist of a red light on the left (port) wingtip, a green light on the right (starboard) wingtip, and a white light on the tail. The aircraft above also has a rotating beacon, an anti-collision light, on top of the tail. The illustration below shows how a pilot can determine the flight direction of another aircraft by reference to the visible position lights.

AEROBATIC FLIGHT (page 102) is not allowed over a congested area, over an open assembly of people, or within certain types of airspace. It may not be performed at less than 1,500 feet above the ground or when the visibility is less than 3 miles. Aerobatics may not be performed while carrying passengers unless each occupant is wearing a parachute. A pilot flying alone is not required to wear a parachute.

DISASTER AREAS consist of airspace in the vicinity of an aircraft or train accident, a forest fire, an area decimated by earthquake, or any other disaster of substantial magnitude. Pilots may not fly into such an area unless they are participating in relief activities or are carrying news personnel. A safe minimum distance is established for each such disaster.

DROPPING OBJECTS from an aircraft is prohibited if it can cause a hazard to people or property on the ground. This does not prohibit dropping an object if reasonable precautions have been taken to avoid injury or damage. Municipal regulations sometimes prohibit dropping leaflets because of the litter problem this can create.

During a preflight inspection, the pilot must inspect the aircraft's propeller *(top)*, **check the engine oil quantity** *(above)*, **and complete other tasks on the aircraft's preflight checklist.**

THE PILOT (pilot-in-command) is the person responsible for the safe operation of the aircraft. During an emergency, a pilot may violate any regulation if doing so is necessary to cope with and resolve that emergency. Prior to any flight, a pilot must become familiar with the available information necessary to conduct that flight safely. This includes a study of weather reports and forecasts, factors involving the airports intended to be used, fuel requirements, and so forth. The pilot also must perform a preflight inspection of the aircraft to ensure that it is in a safe (airworthy) condition.

DOS AND DON'TS

ALCOHOL AND DRUGS are taboo. A pilot must not fly while under the influence of an alcoholic beverage or while using or under the influence of any drug that affects the pilot's ability to fly safely.

SPEED LIMITS must be obeyed even when flying. The maximum-allowable indicated airspeed for any aircraft less than 10,000 feet above sea level is 250 knots (288 mph). There also is a speed limit of 200 knots (230 mph) when flying in the vicinity of airports. No airplane is allowed to fly faster than the speed of sound when over the United States because of the loud and potentially damaging shock waves that this can create.

A STUDENT PILOT, while qualified to fly alone (solo), may not carry a passenger (other than a flight instructor), fly across international borders, or fly for hire or for business. Student pilots may fly only the make and model of aircraft approved by their instructors. If they have not flown during the previous 90 days, they may not solo again until passing a flight check given by their instructor. Students also may not fly beyond the local area near their home airport until authorized by their flight instructor.

A PILOT CERTIFICATE (pilot license) must be in a pilot's possession whenever he or she flies. Pilots also must carry government-issued photo identification (such as a driver's license). They might be required to have a current medical certificate. A radio operator's license is required only when flying outside the United States.

AIRCRAFT CERTIFICATES include an airworthiness certificate, which shows that the aircraft meets government requirements, and a registration certificate similar to that of an automobile. Also required are weight-and-balance data and specific operating limitations applicable to the aircraft. The pilot must determine that all of these certificates are aboard the aircraft. The aircraft registration (license) number is painted on both sides of the fuselage. An "N" preceding the registration number means that the aircraft is registered in the United States; "D" stands Germany, "F" for France, "G" for Great Britain, and so forth.

A PROHIBITED AREA is an area through which a pilot may not fly—it is a *no-fly zone* designed to protect U.S. national security interests such as areas where the president is visiting. Prohibited areas also protect the White House, the Capitol Building, and certain military sites.

TO CARRY PASSENGERS, a pilot must have made at least three takeoffs and landings in a similar aircraft within the previous 90 days. To carry passengers at night, the pilot must have made three takeoffs and landings at night in any type of airplane within the previous 90 days.

CHAPTER 13
LEARNING TO FLY

FLIGHT INSTRUCTION • FIRST SOLO FLIGHT • CROSS-COUNTRY FLIGHTS
WRITTEN EXAMINATION • PRIVATE PILOT CERTIFICATE • THE FLIGHT TEST

FLYING is challenging, exciting, and a great deal of fun. It is not particularly difficult, but a student must be willing to dedicate much effort to study and practice.

A person may take flying lessons at any age but must be at least 16 years old to solo an airplane and at least 17 years old to get a Private Pilot (or Recreational Pilot) Certificate (license). (A student may solo a glider or a balloon at 14 and get a glider or balloon license at 16.) There have been a number of pilots who have learned to fly in their eighties. An initial medical examination is required but is not rigid. For example, a student or private pilot needs a visual acuity of only 20/40 (corrected or uncorrected).

When receiving flight instruction, the student sits in the left seat, and the instructor sits in the right.

FLIGHT INSTRUCTION usually takes place in a small, two-place airplane in hour-long sessions. (Technically, students may learn to fly in any airplane, even a Boeing 767, if they can afford it.) Flight instructors (and all licensed pilots) in the United States must hold pilot certificates issued by the Federal Aviation Administration (FAA).

During the first few hours of instruction, student pilots become familiar with the airplane and the effects of the flight controls. They learn to fly straight and level, and to turn, climb, descend, and glide. Next, they learn slow flight, steep turns, and stalls, and they practice flying around pylons, doing low-altitude S-turns across a road, and making simulated forced landings. As the student becomes competent in these maneuvers and operations, more time is spent practicing takeoffs and landings.

The flight instructor demonstrates how to conduct a preflight inspection *(top)*, which a pilot must do prior to every flight, and briefs the student prior to the first solo flight *(bottom)*.

It is traditional following the first solo flight for the instructor to cut off a piece of the student's shirttail, sign and date it, and then hang it on the wall of the flight school's pilot lounge. This memorializes the event, makes everyone aware of the student's progress, and testifies that he or she has joined the exclusive world of aviators.

THE FIRST SOLO FLIGHT is made by the average student pilot after receiving between 12 and 15 hours of flight instruction. After making a series of takeoffs and landings, the instructor steps out of the aircraft and asks the student to take off, circle the airport, and land unaccompanied. Without the weight of the instructor on board, the airplane will perform much better, which takes many students by surprise. Students are naturally apprehensive during their first solo flight, but practice and experience give them the needed confidence. Celebrations and more hard work follow the first solo.

CROSS-COUNTRY (X-C) FLIGHTS are not flights across the U.S. (although they could be). They are flights between two airports that are at least 50 NM apart. The student learns navigation and cross-country flying after spending solo time practicing takeoffs, landings, and basic flight maneuvers and receiving flight instruction in night and instrument flying. The instructor then takes the student on a triangular flight of 100 to 300 NM with takeoffs and landings made en route at unfamiliar airports. After this, the instructor usually releases the student to make solo cross-country flights, but only along routes and to airports approved by the instructor. One such solo X-C flight must be a triangle with legs totaling at least 150 NM and landings at three airports.

INSTRUMENT FLYING requires a pilot to have special training and knowledge. An advanced license called an Instrument Rating is required for a pilot to enter a cloud, and then only when cleared to do so by air traffic control. Instrument training may be conducted in a simulator that enables a pilot to practice flying solely by reference to his or her instruments without seeing outside the aircraft.

A WRITTEN EXAMINATION must be taken and passed with a minimum score of 70 percent before a student is allowed to take the flight test to become a private pilot. This exam includes the following knowledge areas: (1) the Federal Aviation Regulations, (2) accident reporting regulations, (3) use of certain FAA publications, (4) use of aeronautical charts for navigation, (5) radio procedures, (6) weather situations, reports, and forecasts, (7) aircraft operating procedures, (8) effects of density altitude on aircraft performance, (9) aircraft weight and balance calculations, (10) principles of aerodynamics, engines, and aircraft systems, (11) stall and spin awareness, (12) aeronautical decision-making and judgment, and (13) preflight preparation.

A PRIVATE PILOT CERTIFICATE represents the end of long hours of instruction and practice. To meet the minimum requirements for a license, students must complete at least 40 hours of logged flight time of which a minimum of 20 hours involves flight instruction. Such flight instruction must include at least 3 hours of flight training at night and 3 hours of instrument flight training. Students also must have 10 hours of solo flight (including at least 5 hours of cross-country flying).

After passing the written examination, students must prepare for a flight test during which they must demonstrate proficiency in all of the maneuvers they have been taught and have practiced.

When a student is ready to take the flight test for a license, the student's instructor signs a recommendation stating that he considers the student competent to pass such a test.

Preparing for training at night, which is part of the required instruction for a private pilot certificate.

THE FLIGHT TEST is administered by an FAA-designated pilot examiner. The student must demonstrate knowledge of aircraft certificates, aircraft airworthiness, aircraft performance, loading, checking weather, and planning a cross-country flight. During the flight itself, the student must demonstrate proficiency in performing basic flight maneuvers, cross-country flying, navigation, basic instrument flying, and the procedures needed to handle various emergencies such as a simulated engine failure, a simulated electrical failure, and so forth.

On successful completion of the flight test (also called a practical examination), the student is awarded

a temporary Private Pilot Certificate by the examiner *(above)*. The permanent certificate *(below)* will be sent in the mail. With it, the student can now carry passengers, fly across international boundaries, explore distant horizons, and have more fun than ever imagined.

NOTES

CHAPTER 1
1. "From Benjamin Franklin to Joseph Banks, 30 August–2 September 1783]," *Founders Online*, National Archives, https://founders.archives.gov/documents/ Franklin/01-40-02-0342. [Original source: *The Papers of Benjamin Franklin*, vol. 40, *May 16 through September 15, 1783*, ed. Ellen R. Cohn. New Haven and London: Yale University Press, 2011, pp. 543–552.]
2. Orville Wright, "How We Made the First Flight," *Flying 7*, no. 11 (December 1918): 1062.
3. Napoleon Hill, *The Science of Success* (New York: Penguin Group, 2014).

CHAPTER 3
1. "Perlan 2 glider 76,000 feet world altitude record flight into the stratosphere," MDx media, September 4, 2018, YouTube video, 2:29, https://www.youtube. com/watch?v=KE792Y9hyww; The World Air Sports Federation, "Record: Klaus Ohlmann," accessed April 28, 2022, https://www.fai.org/record/7605.

CHAPTER 10
1. For a detailed key to decoding METARs, see weather.gov/media/okx/Aviation/ TAF_Card.pdf.

IMAGE CREDITS

All credits refer to photos, except those specified as illustrations *(illus.).*
(t = top, b = bottom, l = left, r = right, c = center)

CHAPTER 1

Page 1: Courtesy of San Diego Air and Space Museum. **2–3:** iStock.com/ Mexitographer. **4–5t:** First Flight, by John T. Daniels, commons.wikimedia.org/wiki/ File;First_flight2.jpg, public domain. **5b:** Charles Lindbergh, 1927, National Portrait Gallery, Smithsonian Institution. **6:** U.S. Air Force. **7:** Wiley Post & Winnie Mae, 1933, by Rudy Arnold, National Air and Space Museum Archives, Smithsonian Institution, CC0.

CHAPTER 2

8–9: Courtesy of Textron Aviation. **10–11:** Embraer Aerospace Company. **12t:** Embraer Aerospace Company. **12b** *(illus.):* Scale based on illus. by iStock.com/drogatnev. **15b** *(illus.):* Woman based on illus. by iStock.com/kowalska-art. Man based on illus. by iStock.com/Atlas Studio. **17:** Brian Schiff. **18:** Courtesy of TBM. **19:** Brian Schiff. **20:** Copyright Diamond Aircraft. **24t:** Courtesy of Pilatus Aircraft. **24cl:** Cory W. Watts, flickr.com/photos/63366024@N00/419169715, CC BY-SA 2.0 (creativecommons.org/ licenses/by-sa/2.0/). **25l, 25r:** Brian Schiff. **26t** *(illus.):* Cyclist based on illus. by iStock/ Sudowoodo. **28:** Barry Schiff. **30t:** Aviat Aircraft. **33t** *(illus.):* Man based on illus. by iStock.com/bukavik. **33b:** Courtesy of Pilatus Aircraft.

CHAPTER 3

34–35: Courtesy of Textron Aviation. **36bl:** Raisbeck Engineering. **36br:** Hartzell Propeller. **37t:** Courtesy of Textron Aviation. **37c:** EAA, Vintage Aircraft Association. **37b:** Ryan Fletcher/Shutterstock.com. **38:** Courtesy of Textron Aviation. **39tr, 39tc:** Beriev Aircraft Co. (Russia). **39bc:** Courtesy of Adam Shaw. **39br:** Courtesy Julien Jay. **40t:** Courtesy of Denise Lawton, Soaring Society of America; photo © Steve Hines. **40b:** G. Clivaz, Lange Aviation Gmbh. **42–43t:** Barry Schiff. **42–43b, 43rc:** Courtesy of Lindstrand Balloons. **44tl, 44bl:** Barry Schiff. **44–45c, 45tr:** Goodyear Tire & Rubber. **47t, 47bl:** Robinson Helicopter Co. **47br:** Courtesy of AutoGyroUSA. **48t:** U.S. Navy photo by Mass Communication Specialist 2nd Class Greg Johnson, public domain. **48br:** Photo by Craig Moore, courtesy of www.mooreaircraft.com. **49t, 49bl:** Courtesy of Bell Textron. **50l:** Courtesy of National Oceanic and Atmospheric Administration/ Department of Commerce, photo by Harley D. Nygren, NOAA Corps, 1949. **50–51t, 50–51bc:** Courtesy of Airbus. **51br:** Eduard Marmet, British Airways Concorde G-BOAC, commons.wikimedia.org/wiki/File:British_Airways_Concorde_G-BOAC_03.jpg, CC BY-SA 3.0 (creativecommons.org/licenses/by-sa/3.0/). **52t, 52c:** Pixabay/Wikilmages. **52b:** Mike Fizer. **53t:** Courtesy of Northrop Grumman. **53bl:** Courtesy of Creech AFB, U.S. Air Force photo by Senior Airman Christian Clausen. **54t:** Flight Design USA. **54c:** Courtesy of Kamron Blevins, North Wing. **54b:** Courtesy of Roy Beisswenger, Easy Flight. **55t:** Courtesy of ICON Aircraft. **55c:** Adrian Pingstone (Arpingstone), commons.wikimedia.org/wiki/File:Huntair_pathfinder_mk1_ultralight_g-mjwk_arp. jpg, public domain. **55b:** Courtesy of North Wing Design. **56t:** Courtesy of Hawaiian Airlines. **56b:** Barry Claessens. **57t:** Doug Shane. **57b:** Ben Simon.

CHAPTER 4

58–59: Llstock—stock.adobe.com. **60t:** Reproduced by permission of Lycoming Engines, an operating division of Avco Corporation. All rights reserved. **60b:** Flight Design USA. **62t:** Brian Schiff. **62b:** Aleksandr Lupin/Shutterstock.com. **64t:** Courtesy of ELAFLEX—Gummi Ehlers GmbH. **64b:** www.pipistrel-aircraft.com. **65b:** Brian Schiff. **67t:** Courtesy of Textron Aviation. **67cl**, **67b:** Courtesy of Pilatus Aircraft.

CHAPTER 5

70–71: iStock.com/basslinegfx. **72t:** Brian Schiff. **72b:** iStock.com/RomanSotola. **73t:** Barry Schiff. **73b:** Federal Aviation Administration (FAA). **74tl:** iStock.com/ Eyematrix. **75t:** Brian Schiff. **75br:** Olga Gabay/Shutterstock.com. **76:** Mid-Continent Instruments and Avionics. **78:** Mid-Continent Instruments and Avionics. **80, 81:** Garmin International. **82bl:** mugurel—stock.adobe.com. **83:** Courtesy of TBM.

CHAPTER 6

84–85: Greg Gibson. **86–87, 88–89:** Copyright Diamond Aircraft. **90l:** Courtesy of Pilatus Aircraft. **90–91c:** Courtesy of Dassault Aviation. **91r:** Dr. Norbert Lange/ Shutterstock.com. **93:** Courtesy of NASA. **94:** Jack Snell, American Champion Citabria Adventure (N799K), flickr.com/photos/59972430@N00/10317173473, CC BY-ND 2.0 (creativecommons.org/licenses/by-nd/2.0/). **95:** JetKat/Shutterstock. com **96l:** Pixabay/Pexels. **96–97b:** Beechcraft. **97t:** Aviat Aircraft. **98:** Courtesy of Catalina Island Conservancy. **100t:** Courtesy of Textron Aviation. **100cl:** Redbird Flight Simulations. **102tl:** Photo by Doug Gardner. **102b:** Photo by Glenn Watson. **104:** Photo by Glenn Watson.

CHAPTER 7

106–107: Aviation Supplies & Academics, Inc. (ASA). **108t** *(illus.)*: Globe based on illus. by iStock.com/jack0m. **114:** Barry Schiff. **115:** Aviation Supplies & Academics, Inc. (ASA). **116t, 116b, 117t, 117b:** Dawn Blackman. **119, 121:** Aviation Supplies & Academics, Inc. (ASA). **122c** *(illus.)*: Man based on illus. by iStock.com/Nauma. **122b, 123:** Brian Schiff. **124:** Photo courtesy of Daher.

CHAPTER 8

126–127: United States Government (www.gps.gov). **131t:** Brian Schiff. **131c** *(illus.)*: Woman based on illus. by iStock.com/woojpn. **134b:** Aviation Supplies & Academics, Inc. (ASA). **135:** Brian Schiff. **136t:** iStock.com/igmarx. **136b:** Federal Aviation Administration (FAA). **138t:** USAF, Artist's impression of a GPS Block IIIA satellite in orbit, commons.wikimedia.org/wiki/File:GPS_Block_IIIA.jpg, public domain. **138b** *(illus.)*: United States Government (www.gps.gov). **140t:** Shawn—Airdrie, Canada, flickr.com/photos/cdnav8r/104931620/in/photolist-agNvS, CC BY-SA 2.0 (creativecommons.org/licenses/by-sa/2.0/). **140b:** Dawn Blackman. **141t, 141b:** Garmin International. **142** *(illus.)*: Based on illus. by iStock.com/alphabetMN and iStock.com/loveshiba. **143** *(illus.)*: © Marvin Mutz / Delco Carousel IV-A Inertial Navigation System CDU Illustration, commons.wikimedia.org/wiki/File:Delco_ Carousel_IV-A_Inertial_Navigation_System_CDU_Illustration.png / CC BY-SA 2.0 (creativecommons.org/licenses/by-sa/2.0/).

CHAPTER 9

144–145: Copyright Diamond Aircraft. **146, 147l, 147r, 148:** Courtesy of Pilatus Aircraft. **149:** Ed Hicks. **150:** Courtesy of Pilatus Aircraft. **151:** Dawn Blackman. **152–153:** U.S. Air Force Photo/Dan Hawkins. **153br:** Dawn Blackman. **154l:** David Clark Company. **155:** Moose Peterson.

CHAPTER 10

156–157: Courtesy of Textron Aviation. **158t:** Victoria Hodges. **158b:** Dawn Blackman. **159:** Brian Schiff. **161t, 161b:** Ken Heath. **162l:** Photo by Brandon Morgan on Unsplash (unsplash.com/photos/LHdST1-f2bc). **162–163c:** EF2 tornado near Carpenter, Wyoming, by NWS Cheyenne, commons wikimedia.org/wiki/File:EF2CarpenterWyomingTornado2017.jpg, public domain. **164:** iStock.com/EXTREME-PHOTOGRAPHER. **165cl:** Ivan/Alamy Stock Vector, image ID 2C1AN4G. **166–167c:** Pixabay/flyrtk. **167r:** Pixabay/ccrowder. **168:** Barry Schiff. **171:** Courtesy of Pilatus Aircraft. **172:** Dawn Blackman.

CHAPTER 11

174–175: Courtesy of Pilatus Aircraft. **176tl:** iStock.com/Imageegaml. **176tr:** Bendix/King. **176b:** Courtesy of Pilatus Aircraft. **178l:** LaGuardia Airport Control Tower at Sunset, by Dhaluza, commons.wikimedia.org/wiki/File:LGA_C1_sunset.jpg, CC BY-SA 3.0 (creativecommons.org/licenses/by-sa/3.0/) **178–179tc:** Photo courtesy Airservices Australia. **179tr:** U.S. Air Force photo/Senior Airman Christine Halan. **179bc:** iStock.com/gorodenkoff **180l:** Blythe Airport California, by TomLozeThwaite, commons.wikimedia.org/wiki/File:Blythe_Airport_California.jpg, CC BY 3.0 (creativecommons.org/licenses/by/3.0/). **180–181c:** Pixabay/sipa. **182:** Courtesy of the U.S. Geological Survey. Visit the USGS at https://usgs.gov. **183:** Federal Aviation Administration (FAA). **186–187b** (*illus.*): Man based on illus. by iStock.com/bukavik. **187t:** Jaroslav Francisko/Shutterstock.com. **189:** Vans RV-7 (G-KELS) at Kemble Airfield, Gloucestershire, England, by Arpingstone, commons.wikimedia.org/wiki/File:Vans.rv-7.g-kels.arp.jpg, public domain.

CHAPTER 12

190–191: Cirrus Aircraft. **192:** Courtesy of ICON Aircraft. **193:** Pixabay/jplenio. **194:** Courtesy of Pilatus Aircraft. **195:** F/A-18C Hornet, U.S. Marine Corps photo by Cpl. Nicole Zurbrugg, commons.wikimedia.org/wiki/File:VMFA-122_completes_Pitch_Black_qualified,_ready_160817-M-OH021-2438.jpg, public domain. **196–197t:** Dawn Blackman. **196bl:** Brian Schiff. **197b:** Embraer Emb-500 Phenom 100 Arcus Air, by Laurent ERRERA from L'Union, France, commons.wikimedia.org/wiki/File:Embraer_Emb-500_Phenom_100_Arcus_Air_(AZE)_D-IAAW_-_MSN_50000245_(10223104476).jpg, CC BY-SA 2.0 (creativecommons.org/licenses/by-sa/2.0/).

CHAPTER 13

198–199: Maksym Dragunov—stock.adobe.com. **200:** www.pipistrel-aircraft.com. **201tl, 201bl, 201r:** Dawn Blackman. **202t:** Mike Jesch. **202b:** Brian Schiff. **203t:** Dawn Blackman. **203c:** Barry Schiff. **203b:** Cirrus Aircraft.

ABOUT THE AUTHOR, 212: Mike Fizer

The appearance of U.S. Department of Defense (DoD) visual information does not imply or constitute DoD endorsement.

INDEX

The author wishes to express his grateful appreciation for the dedicated contribution of ASA's talented production team: Kelly Burch, Graphic Designer; Laura Fisher, Editor; James Johnson, Director of Aviation Training; and Jackie Spanitz, General Manager.

ABOUT THE AUTHOR

BARRY SCHIFF has received worldwide recognition for his wide-ranging aeronautical accomplishments and has logged 28,000 hours in more than 363 types of aircraft. He was a rated Airline Transport Pilot at age 21 and has earned every FAA category and class rating (except airship) and every possible instructor's rating. Schiff retired from Trans World Airlines in 1998 after a 34-year career during which he flew everything from the Lockheed Constellation to the Boeing 747.

He holds five world speed records and has received numerous honors for his many contributions to aviation safety. These include a Congressional Commendation, the Louis Bleriot Air Medal (France), Switzerland's Gold Proficiency Medal, and an honorary doctorate from Embry-Riddle Aeronautical University. Schiff also has been inducted into the National Flight Instructor's Hall of Fame, elected as an Elder Statesman of Aviation by the National Aeronautic Association, and inducted as a Living Legend of Aviation.

An award-winning journalist and author, he is well known to flying audiences for his numerous books and more than 1,800 articles published in 111 aviation magazines, notably *AOPA Pilot* of which he currently is a contributing editor.

In 1995 and with the direct approval of Jordanian King Hussein and Israeli Prime Minister Itzhak Rabin, Schiff contributed to the Middle East peace process by leading a formation of 35 airplanes carrying 135 Americans, Israelis, and Jordanians from Jerusalem to Amman. As a result, he became the first pilot ever allowed to fly between those countries.

These credentials have not diminished his passion for flying light aircraft, which he has used to span oceans and continents.